King RICHARD II

This Book Belongs To
Mary Louise Heiser
February 1997

Cover picture: *Richard II with patron saints. "The Wilton Diptych" c. 1395*

King
RICHARD II

BRYAN BEVAN

The Rubicon Press

The Rubicon Press
57 Cornwall Gardens
London SW7 4BE

First published 1990
Reprinted 1996

British Library Cataloguing in Publication Data

Bevan, Bryan
King Richard II.
1. England. Richard II, King of England
I. Title
942.038092

ISBN 0-948695-17-X

Designed and typeset by The Rubicon Press

Printed and bound in Great Britain by Biddles Limited of
Guildford and King's Lynn

Contents

List of illustrations

Acknowledgements

To His Grace, Hugh late Duke of Northumberland for kindly allowing me to consult the archives at Alnwick Castle.

To Jennifer Rankalawson of the National Portrait Gallery, London for her helpful advice concerning illustrations.

To the Trustees of the Bodleian Library, Oxford for the trouble they took over matters of research, particularly in relation to Richard in Ireland and in showing me an illuminated MSS that had belonged to the King.

Once again to my friend Andrew Low for arranging that I should stay in New College, Oxford and for accompanying me to North Wales, Chester and Leeds Castle, Kent.

To Mr. Charles Legh of Adlington, Cheshire for supplying me with photocopies about his ancestor, Sir Peers à Legh, a trusty friend of Richard II, who lost his life in his service.

Once again to the London Library for their help and constant courtesy.

To the Keeper of the Muniments, Westminster Abbey and to the Librarians for their help.

Once again to my publishers Anthea Page and Juanita Homan of The Rubicon Press for their encouragement in this venture so vital for an author, and for their help.

Preface

Richard II, who succeeded his grandfather Edward III as King in 1377, is one of the most important and controversial of the medieval Plantagenet sovereigns. The name 'Plantagenet' is derived from their ancestor Count of Anjou who wore in his hat a sprig of broom (*genêt* in French, *planta genista* in Latin), originally adopted as a gesture of humility during a pilgrimage to the Holy Land. It was later used as the Angevin family crest. My purpose in writing a new study is to give a balanced portrait of the gifted Richard and to reject the biased distortions of the contemporary Lancastrian Chroniclers. It is far from an easy task to delve into the Chronicles, both Yorkist and Lancastrian to ascertain how far Richard's character has been maligned. Shakespeare's *Richard II* is magnificent drama, and even accurate in some respects, but it is fatal to conceive of it as history. His reign of twenty-two years is surely one of the most dramatic in our long, island history. Strange new forces were at work, unleashed in the Peasants' Revolt or People's Revolution (1381), an important date in our medieval history. It marked an epoch of frightening social unrest when Englishmen first became aware of their rights. Richard certainly never regarded himself as a Constitutional King. He was no democrat. His ultimate aim was to establish a régime of royal absolutism, restoring monarchy as he conceived it, to its rightful place in the Kingdom. That he ultimately failed was largely owing to the vast, vested interests of too powerful barons whose hostility he had incurred.

By temperament Richard was a peacemaker, unlike his father the Black Prince and his grandfather Edward III, who had whetted and fired the imagination of their contemporaries and posterity by the victories at Crécy and Poitiers. It was his misfortune to be born during the Hundred Years War, those devastating wars with France, which actually lasted from the late 1330s to the early 1450s, despite long periods of truce. It had started during the reign of Edward III, caused by economic rivalry between England

and France, the inter-relation between the two countries and the problems of the succession.

Richard succeeded to the throne as a boy king at a period when England was undergoing economic and political change. Feudalism, introduced by William the Conqueror, was beginning to break down, though its pattern of land-ownership and occupancy was to endure for many years. Gradually, during the late fourteenth century, it became customary for a peasant, bound to his lord as a 'villein', to commute this service to rent. Then there was the gradual breakdown of the manor unit with its system of strip cultivation. After the Black Death in 1348-49 had reduced England, a nation of perhaps four million people to perhaps two million, five hundred thousand, the market value of labour had been doubled at a stroke, according to Trevelyan. The catastrophe had encouraged labourers to fight for better wages and given the impulse to 'villeins', pursuing lives of compulsory labour on their lords' estates, to throw off their chains.

Yet England was prosperous enough, owing to the importance of the wool trade, of great significance in Richard II's reign and that of his grandfather, particularly in East Anglia. The industry was well organized and ancient, known as the 'staple', a kind of continuing market whereby wool and woolfells produced in England had to be inspected, taxed and sold. In the thirteenth century, various important English towns held the staple, which were later held in the Low Countries and finally at the end of the century in Calais. The wealth of one important magnate, the Earl of Arundel, was largely derived from the lucrative trade.

The most powerful section in the community was undoubtedly the great magnates, whose influence was on a national scale. There were the ancient nobles, the Fitzalans, Earls of Arundel, the Beauchamps, Earls of Warwick, the Mowbrays, the Staffords, and in the North, the Percies and Nevilles, all jealous of their hereditary rights as the natural advisers of their young king. Many were immensely wealthy, possessing annual incomes of between £60,000 and £90,000. On a lower scale were the knightly class, whose influence was mainly local rather than national.

In the later fourteenth century we must bear in mind the growing importance of the middle class, the so-called burgesses, described as townsmen increasingly conscious of their rights within their communities. Typical officials were the reeves or sheriffs, and the Miller, so vividly depicted by Chaucer in *The Canterbury Tales* (The Prologue).

> The Reeve was a slender, fiery-tempered man
> He shaved as closely, as a razor can.

The Miller, too, is so alive

> His big-beefed arms and thighs . . .
> He was a thick, squat-shouldered lump of sins.

In my book I have much to say about Richard's civilized tastes and the artistic importance of his reign. His deposition was in many ways a great tragedy, for the English Renaissance would have surely come earlier if he had remained King. What eventually succeeded his untimely death were many years of strife, the bloody Civil Wars of York and Lancaster terminating in the ascent to the throne of our first Tudor sovereign, Henry VII, in 1485.

I   The Londoners' King

Prince Richard, younger son of Edward Prince of Wales or Edward of Woodstock, was born at Epiphany on January 6th 1367 in the Abbey of Bordeaux. The first known mention of Edward the Black Prince, eldest son of Edward III, as he is familiarly called today, occurred in *Grafton's Chronicle*[1] (1569) in the days of the First Elizabeth. The Black Prince was a man of magnificent tastes, famous not only as a great warrior, but renowned for his chivalry in warfare, his spontaneous generosity, and his magnanimous treatment of his prisoners. "Let the boy win his spurs," his proud father had exclaimed at Crécy when the Prince of Wales was sixteen. The glamour of his personality clings to him even today when we think of the victor of Poitiers and of Najéra during the wars with France. Richard's mother, Princess Joan, was the Black Prince's cousin, younger child of Edmund of Woodstock,[2] Earl of Kent, a son of Edward I by his second marriage to Margaret of France. According to her contemporary, the Chronicler Jean Froissart, she was *"en son temps la plus belle de tout le roiaulme d'Angleterre et la plus amoureuse"*. Because of her surpassing beauty she was later known as "the Fair Maid of Kent". It is evident that the Black Prince's marriage to Princess Joan was a genuine love match, but he was already over thirty when he married her at Lambeth in the presence of Edward III, Queen Philippa and all the royal family. It would have been surprising if Joan had not had many suitors, and her first husband, Sir Thomas Holland, had already died when the Black Prince started a liaison with his widow, which culminated in their marriage. She was born in 1328, and was consequently two years older than her husband, by no means unintelligent, warm-hearted by nature, tactful, devoted to her younger son Richard and later, a wise mediator in his relations with others. Was the Black Prince jealous of his wife's many amours? It is certainly possible.

Now by the Treaty of Brétigny (1360), France was to be divided into two countries. While Edward III and his successors were to have an enlarged Aquitaine and hold Ponthieu and greater Calais in full sovereignty, the King and his eldest son released all claims over Normandy, Anjou, Maine, Brittany and Flanders. Then two years later, King Edward, always generous to the Black Prince, allowed him to set up his Court at Bordeaux and rule the country with his own officers and administration, completely free from interference by the English Court. At Bordeaux and Angoulême, he kept a splendid Court, but he was very extravagant, a fault inherited by his son Richard. Both father and son possessed magnificent taste in art and a special love of jewelry. Fearful that one day he would get into debt, he bought a fine ruby worth £1,883.6.8, intending to sell it, if necessary. Every day 80 knights and 320 esquires had to be fed at his table, and constant jousts and tournaments were held at Bordeaux and Angoulême, similar to those in London and Windsor.

Richard was only three days old when christened in the Cathedral of Bordeaux, his Godfathers being James III, the Titular King of Majorca, and the Bishop of Agen. It is curious that Jean Froissart, the great Chronicler, was in Bordeaux at this time. He relates that Sir Richard Pontchardor, then Marshal of Aquitaine, made a strange prophecy concerning Richard, predicting that he would be a King, though his elder brother Edward of Angoulême, the Black Prince's favourite son, was still alive.

Much later, when writing about Richard's downfall, Froissart related some rumours that he was the son of a handsome French clerk or canon, not the Prince of Wales, an absurd story because there is no evidence whatsoever that Joan was unfaithful to her husband. Much was made of Richard's alleged lack of resemblance to the Black Prince, though his early Archbishop of Canterbury, Simon Sudbury, so foully murdered during the Peasants' Revolt, said that Richard as a young man was the image of his father, the Prince of Wales. The Lancastrian Chronicler, Adam of Usk, no friendly critic, relates that Richard was "fair among men even as another Absalom". The infant Richard inherited French blood both through his father's family and that of Princess Joan, and he had an instinctive feeling for that country, though he was later harshly criticized by the barons for seeking peace rather than war. For many people, Richard was an enigma.

In his infancy, Richard's nurse, Mundina Danos of Aquitaine would rock her Prince's cradle and in her soft, lilting voice sing ballads of Crécy and Poitiers, for ever immortalized by his father. The Black Prince can have seen little of his younger son, for Richard was only three months old when his father and his uncle, John of Gaunt (Ghent) invaded Spain through the Pass of Roncesvalles to support Pedro the Cruel, legitimate ruler of Castile in his fight against Henry of Trastamara, who had temporarily succeeded in banishing Pedro from his Kingdom. Henry of Trastamara had powerful allies, which included the armies of Charles V of France, led by Bertrand du Guesclin, an eminent soldier of genius. Then at Najéra, on April 3rd 1367, not far from Pampeluna, the Black Prince gained the last of his great victories against the French and Castile, taking du Guesclin prisoner. After Najéra, misfortunes pursued the Prince of Wales for the rest of his life. He sickened with dysentery, and was now a very ill man. It is possible to understand, but not to justify, the blemish on his name when he ordered the terrible massacre at Limoges (1370).

In January 1371, his favourite eldest son, Edward of Angoulême died, and Prince Richard as his surviving heir became of more importance. During the impressionable, first nine years of his life, Richard undoubtedly felt overshadowed by the personality and illustrious name of his father, much as he admired him. It was a difficult heritage. Of slender build, and revealing at an early age, a mental aptitude for artistic pursuits, the Prince was never intended by nature to be a great soldier, though constantly exhorted by those around him to follow his father's example. However, it must be said that from an early age Richard never lacked either mental or physical courage.

The Black Prince made, on the whole, a wise choice in appointing Sir Simon Burley and Sir Guichard d'Angle his son's tutors when he returned to England. Both were old companions in arms. The two most significant influences on Richard in his boyhood were his mother, Princess Joan, and Sir Simon Burley. By 1372, Burley was aged thirty-six, a fine soldier, schooled in diplomacy on a mission to Pedro of Castile, and a man of wide culture. He pos-

3

sessed a library containing twenty-one books, all in French except a romance in English. He became absolutely devoted to his young master, and Richard, in turn, was always loyal and generous to Burley, for one of his finest qualities was his loyalty to his friends. Sir Simon being a devoted royalist, would have encouraged his royal pupil to possess a lofty conception of the royal prerogative. Jean Froissart describes his other tutor Sir Guichard d'Angle as "merry, true, amorous, sage, secret, large, experienced, hardy, adventurous and chivalrous".

The Prince of Wales became a very sick man during the early 1370s, living mostly with his wife Princess Joan at Berkhamstead Castle in Hertfordshire. King Edward III, whose reign of fifty years had been so glorious, was slowly dying, so it seemed more than likely that his grandson would succeed him. Burley would have instructed Prince Richard in all the noble virtues, concentrating on making him a worthy medieval knight, a skilled jouster and horseman, brave and hardy. It is evident that his tutor's training gave Richard a taste for books. The King later possessed a dozen books of French romances, including one of King Arthur, and another one of Perceval and Gawyn. Froissart later relates that Richard spoke French extremely well. However, his boyhood was very lonely, for he had few companions of his own age. An early friend was Thomas Mowbray (Twelfth Baron), about a year older than Richard. Another early companion was Ralph Stafford, son and heir of the Earl of Stafford, a lad tenderly loved by Richard in his youth, according to the Monk of Westminster. His most intimate and congenial friend was Robert de Vere.

The early Plantagenet Kings were very fortunate in their Queens, for Eleanor of Castile, Edward I's Spanish-born first wife and Philippa of Hainault, Richard's grandmother, were outstanding women. After Queen Philippa's early death in 1368 (she was Froissart's early patroness), Edward III's character deteriorated, for he fell entirely under the influence of his mistress Alice Perrers, daughter of a prominent Hertfordshire landowner, married to Sir William de Windsor. It was whispered at Court that Alice's domination of Edward III was owing to her restoring his sexual potency through the sorcery of a friar expert in the occult arts. With an eye to the main chance, she became exceedingly wealthy. The long reign of Edward III was slowly ending, as inglorious as it had once been splendid.

While the people were dazzled by the series of brilliant victories such as Crécy, Poitiers and Najéra, they did not complain about the burden of taxation, but the failure of the military campaigns in France in the early 1370s caused great discontent and unrest. Much of the blame they laid on the shoulders of John of Gaunt, Richard's uncle and Edward III's fourth son, who had served abroad with his elder brother, the Black Prince.

Posterity has regarded the powerful, influential nobleman, the Duke of Lancaster, more sympathetically than in his own age. Shakespeare's elder statesman, "time-honoured Lancaster" was widely mistrusted by many of his contemporaries, and almost certainly, unjustly suspected of designs on his father's throne after his death, thus threatening his nephew's inheritance. John of Gaunt's vast influence was largely owing to his position as a great feudal landowner. Much of his wealth had been acquired through his first marriage to the lovely Blanche of Lancaster, daughter of Henry, Duke of Lancaster, a great soldier and Edward III's cousin. Blanche, as described by Froissart, must have been enchanting, "gay and glad she was, fresh and sportive, sweet, simple and of humble semblance, the fair lady whom men called Blanche". A great poet, Geoffrey Chaucer, was inspired after her early death (1369) to write his *Book of the Duchess*.

John of Gaunt owned the magnificent Palace of the Savoy in London and Kenilworth Castle in Warwickshire with its exquisite, delicate banqueting hall, perhaps the most beautiful piece of domestic architecture in medieval England. Its barbaric grandeur, however, hardly fitted it to be the Palace of a great nobleman. He also owned many other castles: Dunstanburgh in Northumberland, Leicester, Nottingham, Monmouth, Skenfrith and Lancaster.

The Duke of Lancaster was thirty-six in 1376, the year before Prince Richard's accession, arrogant, proud, a poor soldier, but clever diplomat, and possessing a characteristic contempt for the Commons when they dared to defy the Court party. "What do these base and unnoble Knights attempt?" he said to his friend, Henry Percy, Lord of Alnwick Castle, who was later to quarrel with him. He was intensely ambitious, but his aspirations, after

1371, lay abroad in Castile rather than in England. During September he married Constanza, heiress of Castile, second daughter of Pedro I of Castile and Leon, now Duchess of Lancaster. His own title of 'King of Castile and Leon' was at least dubious. Constanza never really identified herself with her adopted country.

To understand the situation in England before Prince Richard became boy King, it is essential to discuss the proceedings of the so-called Good Parliament (1376). When their able Speaker, Sir Peter de la Mare, a Knight of the Shire for the County of Hereford and Steward to the Earl of March, was invited on behalf of the Commons, sitting in the Painted Chamber at Westminster, to vote substantial subsidies for the prolongation of the war and to provide for the good government of the country, he insisted most firmly that redress of grievances must precede supply. Two of the King's Ministers, William Lord Latimer, Chamberlain to Edward III, and Richard Lyon, a London merchant, were impeached, accused of embezzling public money. Whether or not they were guilty it is impossible to say but Latimer was deprived of his place at Court and put under arrest, while Lyons was imprisoned. Nobody was sorry when in her turn, Edward III's rapacious mistress, Alice Perrers was strongly attacked in Parliament. She had openly connived at the interference of justice, enriching herself in the process. To attack the royal mistress was tantamount to vilifying the King, but the Commons insisted that her property should be confiscated. She must be exiled from Court.

There now died at the Palace of Westminster (June 8th) Richard's father, the heroic Black Prince, to be given a magnificent funeral in Canterbury Cathedral. A fierce, proud, yet strangely humble man, passionate by nature, unforgiving, and subject, like his son, to those terrible Plantagenet rages. There is the bitter frustration and despair of the heir to the throne. "Where is now my great beauty? My flesh is wasted". By the death of his father, Richard now a boy of nine, became of even more importance.

It is impossible to defend John of Gaunt's rashness in declaring the Acts of "The Good Parliament" as null and void, in restoring the dismissed Ministers and permitting Alice Perrers to return to Court. Even more reprehensible were his orders that Peter de la Mare should be imprisoned in Gaunt's castle at Nottingham.

William of Wykeham, a Bishop of immense influence and erudition, who had remorselessly attacked John of Gaunt's friend Lord Latimer, was to be deprived of his temporalities. For the time being, William of Wykeham was disgraced, forbidden to come within twenty miles of the Court. As a political opportunist, John of Gaunt's own religious sympathies inclined towards the teachings of the great religious reformer, John Wyclif as did those of his sister-in-law, Princess Joan, whose relations with her brother-in-law were excellent.

On his death-bed, the Black Prince may have feared lest his surviving son Richard should be deprived of his inheritance, for he entrusted him to the personal protection of his father Edward III. In leaving Richard the greater part of his property, he swore a solemn medieval oath that the boy would be cursed if he ever gave it away. That the Black Prince suspected John of Gaunt of malevolent designs against his nephew is unlikely since he appointed Gaunt the first executor of his will.

Richard was nearly nine in November 1376, when created Prince of Wales, Duke of Cornwall and Earl of Chester. Then on Christmas Day, the old King made it absolutely clear to his sons the Duke of Lancaster, to Edmund of Langley, Earl of Cambridge and to his youngest son Lord Thomas of Woodstock that his grandson should be King after his death. Not only was Richard granted the confiscated property of William of Wykeham, but the King made him sit at table "above all his own children in great estate". This was an important ceremonial occasion in Westminster Palace. From the first, after the death of his father, self-seeking flatterers would swarm round young Richard. He was never allowed to be young. On one occasion at the end of January (1377) the citizens of London gave a splendid civic reception for the Prince when fountains spurted wine in Cheapside. How bewildering the scene must have been at the magnificent banquet, while he watched the medieval mumming and dancing.

That winter, a few months before the accession of Richard II, the London mob were in turbulent mood forcing his uncle, John of Gaunt, to flee for his life to join his nephew and his sister-in-law, Princess Joan, in the Royal Palace of Kennington. When Gaunt tried to protect John Wyclif, the reformer, at his trial for heresy before William Courtenay, Bishop of London, he together with Lord Henry Percy, angered the citizens of London by tactlessly bringing into old St. Paul's Cathedral their armed retainers. The first followers of Wyclif were known as Lollards, derived from the middle Dutch word *lollen*, applicable to those who muttered or mumbled their prayers. Wyclif had antagonized many bishops and leaders of the orthodox church, pursuing lives of ostentatious luxury by advocating that both clergy and laymen should follow the meek and charitable life of Jesus. Many influential people, including Princess Joan, Prince Richard's mother and John de Montague, Third Earl of Salisbury, favoured the reformer. He had many sympathizers in the City of London. His trial broke up with rioting and in the confusion, he managed to escape to the comparative peace of Oxford. It was with a sense of great uneasiness and dismay that Princess Joan, fearful for her beloved son's heritage and knowing that King Edward was sinking fast, watched John of Gaunt's barge moving rapidly towards Kennington.

On St. George's Day 1377, at a spectacular ceremony in Windsor Castle, Prince Richard was created a Knight of the Garter. Earlier, John of Gaunt persuaded his father to make his Dukedom of Lancaster by Royal Charters February 28th, a Palatinate for his life. The old King did not realize the significance of his act. It was to have fatal consequences for his grandson Richard twenty-two years later, for a later Charter (February 16th 1390) during Richard's reign enacted that these powers were entailed with the title of Duke of Lancaster upon John and his heirs male for ever.[3] These powers and privileges now became hereditary.

Richard was aged ten when his grandfather, in his dotage a despised King, died on June 21st 1377 at Sheen Palace. Edward is at least fortunate that he is remembered in his days of glory, for Sluys and Crécy rather than his ignominious end. Whether or not Alice Perrers stripped the rings off the fingers of the dying man is uncertain, but such an act would be characteristic of her avarice.[4]

Richard now ascended the throne as Richard II. Many people, including Adam of Usk, a lawyer by profession and a chronicler with Lancastrian sympathies, were fearful for the new reign, the advent of a boy King. He quoted the well-known line from Ecclesiastes: "Woe to thee, O land, when thy King is a child". Yet

8

Richard's grandfather had succeeded to a troubled kingdom at the age of fifteen, and had reigned at least for forty years with success.

The nobles, first of all called Richard 'The Londoners' King', and he was loved because of their great affection for his father's memory. Richard was later such a great patron of the Abbey Church of Westminster and of Westminster Hall that he was aptly named. He is also known as Richard of Bordeaux, his birth-place in France, and the title of a celebrated play by Gordon Daviot (1932).

Prince Richard with his mother was staying in Kingston-upon-Thames just before King Edward's death, when a delegation of the citizens waited on the heir to the throne to beg him to come to London, so as to mediate in the quarrel between the City and the Duke of Lancaster. At the Palace of Sheen, surrounded by his family, the boy King received his Uncle. No longer arrogant, he fell on his knees, imploring his nephew to compose the dispute between the magnates and himself. Richard succeeded in settling the dispute between the Duke of Lancaster and William of Wykeham. He ordered that the courageous Speaker of the Commons, Sir Peter de la Mare should be released from prison.

The period just before Richard's coronation was an unsettled, unhappy one for England. The fleets of France and Castile harried the ports and coves of Southern England, overrunning the Isle of Wight, while the Scots as ever troublesome, made incessant raids over the border.

Richard II's coronation in Westminster Abbey on July 16th 1377 was a day of magnificent pageantry for ever memorable, but an exhausting ordeal for the boy King. It has been described in great detail by Abbot Littlington, an outstanding Abbot of Westminster, in a book in the custody of the Deans of Westminster.[5] On the day preceding the coronation, the King rode in his cavalcade from the Tower, through Cheapside, Fleet Street and the Strand to Westminster. The tradition continued for nearly three hundred years until after the coronation of Charles II. We hear now of the Knights of the Bath, a Degree of Knighthood in medieval times, not an 'Order'. These were favourite companions of the King, escorting Richard to his Palace of Westminster. In 1725, King George I by Letters Patent created a military Order of Knighthood.

It is not difficult to imagine the awe of the boy Richard, the love of pomp and decorum early imbued in his mind, his delight in the beauty of the music, and the mystic sense in the solemn ritual. Above all, Richard was not too young for the anointing ritual to pervade his mind with a conception of the 'Divine Right of Kings'. Scarlet cloth had been laid down by William de Latymer, the King's almoner, from the hall of the Palace of Westminster to the Abbey. So the boy Richard, wearing white robes and a pair of red velvet shoes with *fleur-de-lis* worked on them in pearls, passed in his procession to the Abbey. Preceding the King came the Duke of Lancaster, bearing the sword 'curtana'. As Lord High Steward, he had an important part to play. The Earls of March and Warwick followed with the second sword and the gilt spurs, while his younger uncles Edmund of Langley, Earl of Cambridge, and Lord Thomas of Woodstock (then aged twenty-two) both bore a sceptre surmounted with a dove.

Simon Sudbury, Archbishop of Canterbury crowned the King, assisted by the Bishops of London and Winchester. When seated in the Coronation Chair, the Barons of the Cinque Ports held over him a square awning or canopy of purple silk resting on four silvered staves, ornamented with bells of silver gilt. As the exhausted boy had to be carried back to the Palace of Westminster on the strong shoulders of his tutor Sir Simon Burley with the crowds milling all around him, he lost one of his red velvet shoes. On March 10th 1390 - thirteen years later - the King sent a pair of red shoes with *fleur-de-lis* worked on them in pearls to the Abbey. They had been blessed by Pope Urban VI shortly before his death.

The Monk of Westminster, author of *The Westminster Chronicle*,[6] voices strong criticism, maintaining that the King should go to the vestry and don other garments laid out ready for him by his Chamberlains before returning to the Palace. To blame a boy of eleven years for his thoughtlessness hardly seems fair in the prevailing circumstances.

Before attending the Coronation Banquet in Westminster Hall, the King made four grants of peerage. Thomas of Woodstock, his youngest uncle, was created Earl of Buckingham, his tutor Guichard d'Angle, Earl of Huntingdon, his early friend Thomas Mowbray, Earl of Nottingham, and Henry Percy, the Lord Marshal,

Earl of Northumberland, probably owing to the influence of John of Gaunt. The Earl's eldest son, Harry Percy, a boy of eleven, destined to be the famous Hotspur, was at the same time knighted. Three days later a great Council was appointed by the King's advisers, excluding the Duke of Lancaster and the new Earl of Buckingham, but including the Earl of Cambridge, a man too indolent to have any real influence, Ralf Erghum, Bishop of Salisbury, John of Gaunt's Chancellor, Courtenay Bishop of London, Richard Fitzalan, Earl of Arundel and others. This in effect was a Council of Regency, but its members did not work harmoniously together because of their rivalry. A policy of drift and inaction prevailed. Behind the scenes, the influence of Princess Joan, the Queen-Mother was paramount. John of Gaunt wisely remained in the background for the time being, and in consequence retained his influence, retiring to his estates at Kenilworth.

England had seldom been more humiliated than in the first months of Richard's reign. The admirals of France and Castile cheekily invaded the South Coast, burning the little town of Rye - a Cinque Port, Rottingdean and Hastings, taking the Prior of Lewes as their prisoner. Watchbell Street in Rye, so aptly named, warned residents of the danger when a bell was rung.

Richard's first Parliament was held at Westminster during October 1377, the Speaker being John of Gaunt's old adversary, Sir Peter de la Mare, now freed from prison. In his opening speech, Archbishop Sudbury in the boy King's presence, referred to the noble grace, which God has given you, neither by election, nor by other such way, but only by right of succession of heritage. To the boy intensely listening, it must have seemed that the mystical rites of the Coronation, the unction and the blessing by the Archbishop gave him an ultimate authority, foreshadowing the Divine Right of Kings. Sudbury recommended the boy King to the affection of his subjects.

From the beginning, Richard's reign was dramatic. We do not associate Westminster Abbey with crimes of violence, but an English squire, Robert Hauley was murdered within its sacred precincts during August 1378. It happened thus. Hauley and a fellow squire named Richard Shakel, fighting in the armies of the Black Prince and Sir John Chandos, the best of his generals, had captured a great Spanish nobleman, the Earl of Denia, at the Battle of Najéra. After adjudging that the Earl was Hauley's prisoner, the Black Prince had fixed an enormous ransom. Back in England, Hauley and Shakel kept close watch over their valuable hostage, the Earl's son Alphonso, but the Spanish authorities naturally found his presence as a prisoner an embarrassment. When the squires refused to hand over Alphonso, having been ordered to do so by the Council, they were imprisoned in the Tower. According to one Chronicle,[7] "but the ij squiers dredyng that they sholde lese the ransom of their prisoner, and wolde not brynge him forth atte Kyngis commandaument. Wherefore the Kyng was wroth, and saide that they hadde maad a prison in their own house withynne his reme agens his wille and commandement." Since Richard was only eleven, too young to have strong views about this embarrassing affair, it is absurd to allude to "the Kynge's wrath". Both Hauley and Shakel managed to escape from the Tower, seeking sanctuary in Westminster Abbey. When a letter in the King's name failed to secure the release of the fugitives, Abbot Littlington stoutly maintaining the right of sanctuary, refused to surrender them. Then the Constable of the Tower together with fifty soldiers, Lord Latimer and Sir Rolf Ferrers went to the Abbey monastery on August 11th. They succeeded in capturing Shakel, but Hauley making a desperate resistance was overpowered and killed together with a sacrist named Richard in the Abbey Choir during High Mass. Hauley is buried in Poets' Corner.

The Chronicle says that everybody involved in the murder was excommunicated by the Bishop of London in St. Paul's Cathedral, but he expressly excluded from his curses King Richard, the Princess Joan and the Duke of Lancaster. Armitage-Smith, John of Gaunt's biographer, says in his defence that he had no part in the crime, but was under suspicion by his contemporaries because of his ambition to be King of Castile.

Despite the squalor and the smells there was beauty in medieval London, then a town of 40,000 people, this "flower of cities all", as Chaucer's Scots follower Dunbar named it. Stow's *Survey* gives picturesque details of a mumming in honour of Richard. How gay was the scene in 1377 when "one hundred and thirty citizens disguised and well horsed in a mummerie with sound of trumpets, shackbats, cornets, shalmes (a wind instrument like an oboe) and other minstrels and innumerable torch lights of waxe, rode from Newgate through Cheape over the bridge, through Southwarke, and so to Kennington besides Lambbith, where the young Prince remayned with his mother, the Duke of Lancaster, his uncle, the Earls of Cambridge, Hertford, Warwicke and Suffolke, with divers other Lords."[8]

Cheapside was then an elegant shopping area. The angry citizens set up an effigy of Robert Belknap, Chief Justice of the Common Pleas, there when he firstly denied them their established right to assist the Chief butler during the Coronation Banquet. Always jealous of their rights and privileges, the Londoners took umbrage when Belknap contemptuously told them they might wash up the pots and pans if they liked. In revenge, they ridiculed the Chief Justice by making his figure vomit wine continuously, an early example of caricature in matters political.[9] However, Belknap was forced to give way. The Mayor and Aldermen played their traditional part in the Coronation Banquet.

In Cheapside a citizen could indulge himself in purchasing velvets and silks, and "Parys thred the fynest in the land".[10] At the street corners stood eager tipplers, selling drinks to customers out of little casks. Outside Westminster Hall were the Flemings, many of whom had come to London while Edward III's Queen Philippa of Hainault still lived. Their cries resounded. "Master, what will you buy? Fine felt hat? Spectacles?" At Westminster Gate the cooks cried, "Hot peascots" or "ripe strawberries". The street singers surged, humorous and hardworking. In Candlewick Street, a knowledgeable citizen would resort to buy hot sheep's feet and mackerel. In Smithfield just outside the walls, Earls, Knights and ordinary citizens would repair to buy all manner of horses. Each district of London had its professions, between Queen Street and Bow Lane, the shoemakers and Bucklersbury was famed for its ironmongers.

At first, the Londoners took to their hearts the son of their beloved Black Prince, dazzled by his youth and kingliness, and impressed by his charm and strange, feminine beauty. Of his physical courage they would soon get a proof. Sadly, the citizens were to turn against him later, and the reasons for the alienation can only be understood in the strange drama of his Kingship.

II   The People's Revolt

As he grew to manhood, King Richard became very handsome. His features were delicate, almost feminine, while his hair was fair, rather wavy, reaching below his ears. For most of his life he neither sported a beard nor a moustache, though his portraits give the impression of tufts of light hair falling below his cheeks. Almost six feet tall, his eyes were blue and his fingers long and artistic. He wore the fashionable pointed shoes of the period.

It was unfortunate for the boy King that he was kept too long in subjection by the barons surrounding him. His desperate need to assert himself, to show that he was not an unworthy son of the Black Prince, partly explains his magnificent courage during the Peasants' Revolt (1381), but the most formative early influence in his life together with his marriage to Anne of Bohemia was his mother.

The people had many grievances. There was widespread disenchantment with the Church, intensified by the calamity of the Black Death (1349) during the reign of Richard's grandfather, leading to a serious shortage of labour [1] owing to the death of half the country's population of three or four million. This resulted in a rise in prices, and in an effort to prevent this, successive parliaments had introduced the hated Statutes of Labourers. In these circumstances, the workers were justified in asking for higher wages. Unfortunately, Parliament showed no understanding of the problems facing the country when enacting laws fixing standard wages at rates paid in 1346 (before the Black Death). There were the disillusioned soldiers returned from the wars, no longer sustained by the victories of the Black Prince, given a chilly reception by the people and swelling the ranks of the unemployed.

As Froissart relates - and the historian is at his best - "there occurred in England great disasters and uprisings of the Common people, on account of which the country was almost ruined beyond

14

recovery." It is fair to say, however, that Froissart's sympathies were with the landowning class and not with "the bad people" who rebelled against their masters. The peasants or villeins as they were known, working on the land of their lords, possessed no rights such as representation in Parliament or a free man's rights under the Common Law. Nearly a million men and women were little better than slaves, performing menial services for their lords, tilling his land, baking his bread and brewing his beer for no financial reward. True, there were the better-off villagers possessing holdings of thirty acres in the arable fields, but in return for their holdings under the manorial system then prevailing a paid lander (as they were called) had to work on his lord's land for three or four half-days a week throughout the year, performing various services (ironically known as 'love-loons'), thus allowing him little opportunity to cultivate his own land.

The age of Richard II is an exciting time: the age of Geoffrey Chaucer, Will Langland ('Long Will' as he was nicknamed because he was so tall), Henry Yevele, a great architect, William of Wykeham, now an old man and the impetuous Harry Hotspur, the most famous of the Percies. Langland paints a dark, depressing picture of his age in his scholarly poem, *The Complaint of Piers the Plowman*, forming such a sharp contrast with Chaucer's sense of wonder, human sympathy and love of humanity. 'Long Will' is always mindful of his poverty, singing "placebos" and "dirges" for his living at grand funerals, and daring occasionally to refrain from bowing to the resplendently dressed lords and ladies as they rode so nonchalantly along the Cheap. Never was the contrast between the wealth of the rich and the poverty of the villein toiling in the fields so marked. Langland's poetry roused people to frenzy, influencing them to claim what they considered their rights. How refreshing then to turn to a wonderful passage, a breath of pure merriment, a gleam of light where the dreamer, fretful and weary of the world, falls asleep beside a stream in the Malvern Hills on a glorious May morning. He relates: "I was very forewandered and went me to rest under a broad bank by a burn side, and as I lay and leaned and looked in the water, I slumbered in a sleeping, it sweyred (sounded) so merry."

The influence of John Wyclif, the Oxford scholar, must not be underestimated over his condemnation of the sleek, hypocritical monks with their great bellies. The friars, too, lascivious and pleasure-loving, who seduced the wives and daughters of worthy people. Contemporary satires paint a vivid picture:

> When the good man is from hame
> and the friar comes to our dame
> He spares neither for sin nor shame
> But that he does his will.
> Each man that here shall lead his life
> That has a fair daughter or a wife
> Beware that no friar them shrive.[2]

There were widespread abuses, such as the sale of indulgences. In *The Complaint of Piers the Plowman* we read: "Peter had the keys of heaven and hell, but I trow (know) he never sold sins for money."

The Papacy also was extremely unpopular, all the more so because during the long wars with France in Edward III's reign, most of the Popes were Frenchmen residing in Avignon. Wyclif attacked the Papacy for its rapacity, its simony and shameless sale of indulgences. The hated agents of the Popes, such as the bankers and the lawyers, were the chief tax-collectors of Europe, levying tolls on a country's ecclesiastical revenues.

King Richard was aged eleven in 1378, when an attempt was made to re-establish the Papacy at Rome, much to the alarm of the French cardinals. They established a rival one at Avignon.[3]

The influence of Wyclif's "simple priests", inflaming the minds of the rustics with new ideas of equality, made for social unrest, even revolution. His followers were first known as Lollards. According to Professor Skeat's edition of *The Vision of Piers the Plowman* the sect had begun in Brabant. Gradually Wyclif's followers were to become more diffused and less committed to his teachings. He believed that men should hold a direct relationship with God, thus lessening the importance of the priest as intercessor. Many influential people were attracted by Wyclif's teachings including Richard's mother, Princess Joan, and the boy King's staunch friend John de Montague, third Earl of Salisbury, a cultured, noble man and poet writing in French.

Whether or not John Ball, a priest in Kent, was as "crack-brained" as Froissart alleged,[4] his eloquence certainly incited the mob. His habit was to address the people after mass in the cloisters. "Good people," he cried,

> things cannot go right in England and never will, until goods are held in common, and there are no more villeins, and gentle-folk, but we are all 'unified' [Froissart tout-unis]. In what way are those whom we call lords greater masters than ourselves? How have they deserved it? Why do they hold us in bondage? If we all spring from a single father and mother Adam and Eve, how can they claim or prove that they are lords more than us, except by making us produce and grow the wealth which they spend? They are clad in velvet and Camlet lined with squirrel and ermine while we go dressed in coarse cloth . . . We are called serfs and beaten if we are slow in our service to them, yet we have no sovereign lord we can complain to . . . Let us go to the King - he is young - and show him how we are oppressed and tell him that we want things to be changed or else we will change them ourselves.[5]

They did not blame Richard for their sufferings, but they bore deadly resentment against his advisers. The itinerant friars preached against the excessive wealth in the monasteries. In the ranks of the rebellious villeins were many poor parsons. When the benign Sudbury, Archbishop, heard how John Ball was inciting the people, he had him imprisoned for two or three months, but later released him.

John Ball continued to travel up and down the country sowing sedition, preaching according to the chronicler Walsingham (a monk) of those things which he knew would be pleasing to the common people and speaking evil both of ecclesiastical and temporal lords. Sudbury is usually regarded as weak and inefficient, but at least he had the foresight to have a strong town wall surrounding the Cathedral built at Canterbury (1375-80), for he had good cause to fear mob violence. He shared the cost of it with the people.[6]

What really sparked the people's insurrection was the hated poll-tax introduced by the Parliament meeting at Northampton, during the autumn (1380), for in medieval times the English considered taxes as a form of injustice amounting to robbery. This shilling poll-tax imposed indiscriminately on peasant, alderman or earl bore especially hard on the peasant or town-artisan, not even represented in a Parliament full of lawyers, merchants and prelates. The result might have been foreseen. Throughout Southern England, people hastened to make false tax returns, much to the fury of the government. They seemed strangely insensitive to the resentment aroused by this arbitrary taxation. When tax assessors were instructed to collect the tax in the villages, the people's fury knew no limits. They blamed the Treasurer, Sir Robert Hales ('Hob the robber' as he was called), Archbishop Sudbury, John Legge, a sergeant-at-law, and Richard's unpopular Uncle John of Gaunt, who fortunately for himself, was out of the country engaged in delicate diplomatic negotiations with the Scots. Archbishop Sudbury, now holding the Office of Chancellor, also incurred the hostility of the people.

There are many contemporary accounts of the Peasants' Revolt, varying as they do according to the prejudices of the Chroniclers. Some of the primary sources are *The Westminster Chronicle*, Froissart,[7] the invaluable account in *The Anonimalle Chronicle*, and the more hostile and critical one in *Historia Anglicana*, the work of Thomas Walsingham, a monk of St. Albans Abbey invariably hostile to Richard and John of Gaunt up to 1389, probably because the King favoured Westminster Abbey.

Few things are more terrible than a brutal and illiterate mob let loose to wreak vengeance on their alleged oppressors. *The Westminster Chronicle*[8] relates that "when the main body of rebels from Kent gathered at Blackheath and that from Essex approached London north of the river on June 12th they behaved like the maddest of mad dogs", running wild over much of the country, razing to the ground the manor houses of many landowners, and forcing everybody they met who was not of their fellowship into sworn association with themselves in the defence of King Richard. Since they held themselves up as champions of the King and the welfare of the Kingdom against those who were betraying them,

18

their cry was "for King Richard and the trew Commons". Their quarrel was not with the King, but with the Chancellor Sudbury, the Treasurer Hales, Robert Belknap, Chief Justice, and others.

The leaders of the insurrection were the infamous Wat Tyler, "a tiler of roofs" according to Froissart, "and a wicked and nasty man", and John Ball formerly a priest in York, and possibly in Colchester. Jack Straw was the leader of the Essex insurrection and Tyler undoubtedly possessed military ability. It is doubtful, however, whether he had acquired it during the French wars. It is very possible that he was a convicted robber.

Continuing their bloody course, the rebels after "cutting off the heads of a number of men",[9] pitched their camp at Blackheath where they had a commanding view of London. The villeins and the common people had risen against the power of the state and the ruling class had pursued a policy of masterly inaction. There was a reason for this. The only army in existence at the time of the Revolt was at Plymouth under the Earl of Cambridge, about to embark for Portugal to take part in the Spanish war against France. The boy King and his courtiers were in deadly peril.

According to *The Anonimalle Chronicle*, Richard only fourteen, showed great initiative in dealing with the rebels gathered at Blackheath, suggesting to Wat Tyler a meeting on the banks of the Thames. The King with his mother, his Chancellor Archbishop Sudbury,[10] and several noblemen were in the Tower of London, then a palace as well as a prison, having been escorted there earlier by the Mayor of London, Walworth. It was now that the peasants sent their hostage Sir John Newton, the Governor of Rochester Castle whom they had captured, to the Tower, inviting King Richard to meet them. If he had refused to do so, they would have hacked Newton to death, according to Froissart.

On the morning of Corpus Christi Day (Wednesday June 12th) the young King, after hearing mass in the Tower, attended by the Earls of Salisbury, Warwick and others, was rowed in the royal barge, escorted by four smaller barges to a place near the shore between Rotherhithe and Greenwich where the proposed conference was to take place. From his barge, the King could hear the frenzied cries of the rebels demanding the heads of Sudbury and

Hales who were accompanying him in his barge. He could see two large banners of St. George with its pennants proclaiming 'With whom holdes you? Wyth Kynge Richarde and wyth the Trew Communes.' It seemed as if (Froissart wrote) that all the devils in hell had been let loose. No wonder his entourage counselled prudence, refusing to allow their boy King to land.

Richard was not afraid, calling to them, "Sirs, what have you to say to me? Tell me, I came here to talk to you". They shouted back, rudely, "Come on, land, you! It'll be easier that way to tell you what we want". Salisbury, a hardened warrior, who had fought in many a campaign with Richard's father, answered with a disdainful glance at the rough and tattered clothes worn by the peasants: "Sirs, you are not in a fit condition for the King to talk to you now". Much to the fury of the maddened mob the King rowed back to the Tower. *The Anonimalle Chronicle*[11] describes Richard's bravery, and resourcefulness, and his forgetfulness of self, while his counsellors seemed paralysed by fear. Walsingham, however, criticizes Richard's behaviour when the rebels were encamped at Blackheath. He relates in his *Historia Anglicana* that some of his lords advised the King to hold a conference and that others dissuaded him from doing so. However, he agreed to the counsel of the more prudent lords. Walsingham was always only too ready to impute disreputable motives where the young King was concerned.

After Richard's return to the Tower, the maddened mob chanted: "To London." "Straight to London!" They were perhaps, thirty thousand, swept on by their diabolical impulses, destroying as they pleased the Marshalsea prison, and gleefully setting free the inmates of the Fleet, Westminster and the Newgate gaols to swell the ranks of the insurgents. Far from making any show of resistance, there were many sympathizers among the Londoners eager to appease the violent men with food and drink. Thursday June 13th was a terrible day of rioting and hideous outrages.

The Palace of the Savoy,[12] the London home of John of Gaunt, then in Scotland, was set on fire after all the guards had been killed. In its artistic splendour and beauty it outrivalled the Palace of Westminster. With their leaders Wat Tyler, John Ball and Jack Straw, they swept ever onwards, destroying the Priory of St. John at Clerkenwell. Lustful and revengeful, they delighted in the

20

plunder of the Inns of the lawyers in the Temple just outside the Ludgate. What a rich opportunity it afforded for a citizen, amid the confusion, to take revenge, to harm those he disliked, to mock his enemy by setting up an executioner's block in Cheapside. Perhaps the most brutal outrage was the indiscriminate slaughter of Flemings and Lombards in the City, hated as foreigners, bankers, industrious merchants and money lenders.

Froissart relates that Wat Tyler ordered the rioters to kill a wealthy man named Richard Lyon, his former master. It rankled in his sick mind that he had once flogged him. After Lyon's head was cut off it was pierced with a lance and carried through the streets in triumph.

Richard sat in the Council Chamber in the White Tower in conference with his advisers. They did not lack for experience. There was the second Earl of Salisbury, brave but cautious, knowing the grave issues at stake, the King's half-brothers, sons of Princess Joan, the Earl of Kent and Sir John Holland, the Earls of Warwick and Buckingham Richard's uncle, the Treasurer Sir Robert Hales and the Chancellor Archbishop Sudbury. It was Friday morning. Encamped outside was the rabble in St. Katharine's Square. The boy King could hear their cries threatening that if Richard would not come outside and listen to their grievances, they would storm the Tower by force and kill everyone.

The Council were divided, some urging strong offensive action, while others headed by Salisbury, probably more realistic than William Walworth, the stout-hearted Mayor of London, urged Richard to appease the rioters by fair words. That would be the more prudent course. A promise that everything they sought could later be rescinded on the grounds that it could not be binding when force was employed. After furious argument during the course of which Richard remained calm and courageous, it was eventually decided that Richard should sally forth from the Tower to a conference with the rebels at Mile End, in medieval times an open space where the citizens indulged in various sports. Richard would then agree to all the demands of the rebels in the hope they would disperse to their homes. According to medieval standards, no knight need have a conscience about broken promises to villeins and artisans when the Order of Knighthood lay in such peril.[13] With the cries of the rabble ringing in his ears, one wonders what emotions surged in Richard's bewildered mind as he mounted to a turret and gazed horror-stricken at the City fires. *The Anonimalle Chronicle* relates that he seemed 'pensyve et trist'.

Froissart is incorrect as to timing when he writes that no sooner had the King sallied forth with his nobles than Wat Tyler and the other rebel leaders with four hundred followers stormed their way into the Tower and after seizing the Archbishop and Sir Robert Hales, Treasurer of England and Grand Prior of the Hospital of St. John, instantly beheaded them. Sudbury and Hales were not murdered in the Tower.

As Richard, on horseback, sallied forth with the cavalcade, it is uncertain whether the King's half-brothers, the Earl of Kent and Sir John Holland both considerably older, deserted him or were given a commission to raise help from further afield. Richard's intimate friend, Robert de Vere, was with him, and Aubrey de Vere, Robert's uncle, behaved with great bravery as the boy King's sword-bearer. Richard's mother, Sudbury, Hales, and John of Gaunt's eldest son, Henry of Derby, the King's first cousin then aged about fifteen, were all left behind in the Tower. Walsingham in his Chronicle *Historia Anglicana* savagely attacks the King for abandoning his friends and leaving them to the mercy of the mob. Even his mother was exposed to the insults of the villeins, who made jocular attempts to kiss her. Froissart mentions that the scoundrels tore her bed to pieces, so terrifying the Princess of Wales, a woman of sensitivity, that she fainted. The Monk of Evesham, however, commends Richard II for his courage at Mile End. He relates in his *Historia Vitae et Regni Ricardi II*,

> that when the Lord King had come to the aforesaid place, as he had been commanded, he appeared like a lamb among wolves (indeed he was fearing very much for his own life), and he humbly entreated the people standing there.

Richard and his small party of nobles were confronted by an enormous host of villeins and artisans, hailing from many shires - Froissart mentions 60,000 from Kent, Essex, Bedfordshire, Sussex and Cambridgeshire. He relates the gist of what transpired. When

22

the King rode into their midst, he said: "Good people. I am your Lord and King. What do you want to say to me?" They petitioned him that villeinage should be abolished "so that we shall never again be called serfs or bondmen," demanding that all feudal services should be commuted for a rent of 4d per acre and that a general amnesty and pardon should be granted them. The King and his nobles agreed so willingly to these demands that it is, perhaps, surprising that so many were duped by his promises. Others were more suspicious. Richard, however, ordered thirty clerks to produce instruments of pardon and freedom under the Great Seal. Some of the rebels dispersed, but Wat Tyler, Jack Ball and Jack Straw with many others remained dissatisfied and deeply sceptical.

It was during this vital conference or immediately after it that the murder of the inoffensive Simon Sudbury and Hales took place. St. John's Chapel in the White Tower was, and remains today, an exquisite example of Norman ecclesiastical architecture where Knights of the Bath would pass all-night vigils before being dubbed. From there the Archbishop and Hales, while celebrating mass before the altar, were dragged by ignorant and evil men and instantly beheaded on Tower Green. According to the Monk of Westminster, they nailed on the hallowed head of the Archbishop a scarlet cap. Others to suffer were John Legge, the sergeant-at-arms, and a wretched friar in John of Gaunt's service. Princess Joan for whom the people had a rough affection was borne to the Wardrobe in Carter Lane near Baynard Castle on the Thames, then a royal residence.

Henry, Earl of Derby, was also in St. John's Chapel, but his life was mysteriously and miraculously preserved by a man named John Ferrour of Southwark, who stayed the hand of his would-be assassin. Possibly Ferrour felt gratitude for some favour done him by Henry's father. One thing is certain: the boy never forgot to whom he owed his life. Marie Louise Bruce, in her interesting life of Henry Bolingbroke, blames his cousin Richard "for betraying him, panicking him and agreeing to his death",[14] but the accusation is hardly justified. Richard had ordered both Sudbury and Hales to try to escape from the Tower, even if there was only a slender chance of doing so. In any case, by consenting to the Mile End Conference agreed to by his Council, Richard's own life was also in considerable jeopardy. Real courage is all the more convincing if a boy feels fear.

On the Saturday morning, Froissart relates[15], the King and his entourage left the Queen's Wardrobe on horseback, riding by Ludgate and Fleet Street, past the fearsome ruin of his uncle's Palace of the Savoy, to the Abbey of Westminster. The Monk of Westminster relates that as Richard approached the Monastery Gate, he was met by a procession of the Convent. They had just witnessed a hideous case of sacrilege when Richard Imworth, Steward of the Marshalsea, after fleeing for safety to the Abbey, had been dragged screaming from the columns of the St. Edward Shrine where he clung, to be later beheaded without trial at Cheapside. Richard, we are told, was in tears as he reverently kissed the cross borne before the convent. No medieval King, with the exception of Henry III, held greater affection for the Abbey Church. Richard may be described as an orthodox Roman Catholic, having no sympathy, unlike his mother, with the Lollards.

For a boy of fourteen this was the supreme crisis of his early life, as he kneeled before the sacred shrine, deeply conscious that it was in this holy place, four years ago, that he had been anointed a crowned King. So Richard with his lords, knights and esquires bent their heads in fervent prayer.

Meanwhile, a conference had been arranged between the King and the rebels led by Wat Tyler, Jack Straw and John Ball at Smithfield, then a market. Fearing the violence of the mob - there were, perhaps, over forty thousand rioters present - Richard and his party were wearing shirts of steel beneath their clothes. As they rode towards Smithfield, there was the stench of bodies in the streets and devilish shouts of merriment from the Taverns and Lombards' houses as the mob caroused, giving expression to their xenophobia and drinking the Languedoc wine and malmseys they had stolen. When the King reached the Church of St. Bartholomew the Great, he drew rein. Froissart wrote that the boy King's retinue numbered, perhaps, sixty horsemen.

All the Chronicles have different accounts of Richard's dramatic encounter with his subjects at Smithfield, but all agree as to the insolence of Wat Tyler. The King instinctively acted with authority, ordering Mayor Walworth to summon Tyler to the royal presence.

Leaving his companions, the fellow stuck his spurs into a nag he had mounted, approaching Richard so closely, "that his horse's tail was brushing the head of the King's horse". In the words of the Monk of Westminster, "Their unspeakable leader showed for the King's majesty none of the deference" appropriate for the occasion. Richard required no prompting.

"Why do you not go home?" he asked Tyler abruptly, telling him to relate his demands. The rebel leader replied that nothing would satisfy him except the disestablishment of the Church, only one bishop, and confiscation of Church property for the benefit of the people. Serfage and villeinage must be abolished, and there must be freedom and equality for everybody.

Froissart relates that among the bystanders was John Tickle, a tailor by profession, who had delivered sixty doublets to be worn by the rebels. As if to relieve the mounting tension, he said to Tyler, for like most of his kind it was natural for him to be uneasy as to payment, "I want at least thirty marks". "Be easy now," rejoined Tyler, "you'll be paid in full by tomorrow. Trust me, I can guarantee it".

Richard told Tyler that he was willing to grant him everything possible except his own *régalitée*. It was a warm fine day, and the fellow rudely rinsed his mouth in the King's presence, much to the disgust of Richard and his squires. It so happened that one of the King's retinue, being acquainted with the rebel and knowing his reputation, denounced him as the most notorious thief in Kent.

Taking umbrage at this, Tyler attempted to stab his accuser with his dagger, then turned on the Mayor William Walworth, who had been ordered by the King to arrest him. Fortunately for Walworth, his coat of mail saved him from certain death. The courageous Mayor ran him through the body with his sword. Then a squire named Ralph Standych (according to both the *Knighton Chronicon* and Froissart) seized the rebel leader's head and flung him from his horse to the ground. Unable to see clearly what was happening, some of the rebels even thought that their leader was being knighted by the King. As it dawned on them that Tyler was being murdered, they raised their bows as if to shoot. It was a moment fraught with menace and great danger. Showing supreme courage, Richard rode forward alone, crying, "I am your King, your leader, and captain. Those among you who support me must go into the open country to Clerkenwell Fields."

Wallon, a thoughtful, nineteenth century French biographer of Richard, wrote that "Le jeune roi allait montrer dans cette crise une décision, une presence d'esprit et une vigeur digne du sang de Prince Noir". ("The young King went on to show in this crisis a decisiveness, a presence of mind and a forcefulness worthy of the Black Prince.")

The energetic Mayor Walworth, a member of the influential Fishmongers' Guild, rode through the City summoning the loyal citizens to the aid of the King. Sir Robert Knollys, an experienced soldier, with his men-at-arms together with a wealthy citizen of London, Nicholas Brembre, a Mayor of London (1376-78) drew up in battle formation near the King, who had returned to Smithfield. The loyal troops numbered about seven or eight thousand, but two treacherous aldermen, Sybyle and Horne, had sided with the rebels. When Tyler's gory head, mounted on a lance, was displayed to the rebels at Clerkenwell, soon to replace Sudbury's on London Bridge, they were at last convinced that their cause was hopeless. They fell down on their knees, imploring the King's mercy. Richard then created three new Knights, William Walworth, deeply honoured because he considered himself a mere tradesman, Ralph Standych and Nicholas Brembre. The boy King, supported by the experienced Earl of Salisbury, magnanimously refused to allow Knollys to attack the rebels, although he was boiling for a fight. What really concerned Richard was the recovery of his own banners, so conspicuously displayed by the rebels.

What a joyful reunion with his mother that evening when Joan of Kent tearfully greeted his safe return at the Wardrobe. "Rejoice and praise God, Madame," said the boy King, proudly, "for I have recovered today my heritage which was lost, and the realm of England."

How far Richard can be blamed for duplicity and broken promises to the villeins is hard to say. At Mile End he had ordered thirty clerks to prepare instruments of pardon and freedom under the Great Seal, but these proved completely worthless. Even if the King had the best intentions, his advisers would have ensured that the rebels would suffer harshly for daring to defy their authority.

Richard with his instinctive feeling for the dramatic had revealed aspects of his personality hitherto little suspected. Where his advisers had been mostly supine or even cowardly, Richard had displayed bravery and a sense of responsibility. His gallant behaviour at Mile End, and at Smithfield, signified that the King chafed at his subjection by his decadent barons.

Some historians have seen it as the one spontaneous burst of courage during his life of thirty-three years, but Richard was capable of both moral and physical bravery during the crises of his life.

The Monk of Westminster at first emphasizes the King's distaste for civil bloodshed, his forbearance in not following his military advisers' strong advice that the peasants, after throwing away their weapons - staves, bows and arrows - must be immediately, ruthlessly punished. Certainly the barons were only too willing that Richard should be the scapegoat for their own shortcomings.

When confronted by a deputation of former rebels, asking whether their newly won liberties were valid, Richard is alleged to have used the harsh words: "Serfs, you have been, and are, in bondage and you shall remain - not as heretofore, but incomparably worse."[16] Can one be certain that he ever said these words? Possibly they were put in his mouth by one of his counsellors, furiously resentful that the rebels had dared to defy the government. John Gower, a contemporary writer whose early patron was Richard II, loads Walworth, the Mayor of London, with praise for his gallant conduct at Smithfield, but barely mentions the boy King, a curious lack of generosity. In his Latin poem *Vox Clamantis*, a vision of the Peasants' rising, Gower reflects that, in their lust for what was not their own they had turned into beasts.

In many parts of the country the peasants maintained a stubborn resistance, in St. Albans where they occupied the town and even as far afield as Devonshire. A few of the rebels possessed nobility. A man named Grindecobbe, when offered his life if willing to persuade his followers to restore the Charters wrung from the monks, said bravely: "If I die, I shall die for the cause of the freedom we have won, counting myself happy to end my life by such a martyrdom."[17] The King, accompanied by his uncle, the Earl of Buckingham, and his new Chief Justice Tressilian, made for Essex where the revolt had begun. At Billericay, the inhabitants took to the woods, fighting desperately until finally subdued. Harsh revenge was their portion. Many were hung, drawn and quartered, or died in the field. At St. Albans, there were miscarriages of justice. Tressilian shamelessly browbeat juries, so that fifteen leaders, including John Ball, were brutally executed and many others imprisoned. When the Chief Justice fell into the hands of his enemies seven years later, this was remembered against him.

The rising in Somerset between June 19th and 21st was not of a serious nature, implicating few of the inhabitants of Bridgewater; but Richard was clearly attached to the Charters, showing a reluctance to revoke them until July 2nd, although punitive measures against the rebels began immediately after Smithfield. It gives substance to the view that Richard was ambivalent, willing to free the serfs of his realm when Parliament met four months later. (See Westminster Abbey Draft Letters Patent of Manumission and Pardon for Men of Somerset in 1381.) Richard returned to Westminster, aware how unique was the greatness which pertained to royalty.[18] He was to be sadly disillusioned. For eight long years he was made to pay for his superb behaviour at Smithfield. He learnt how frustrating and impotent he was to exercise the authority of Kingship. How natural for a gifted boy to bitterly resent his subjection by the barons and to complain that his tutelage was unreasonably prolonged.

Dr. Stubbs, in his able summing-up of the repercussions after the Peasants' Revolt,[19] errs when he writes: "Although villeins had failed to obtain their Charters and had paid a heavy penalty for their temerity in revolting, they had struck a vital blow at villeinage." True, economic development continued, but it was very gradual. The break-up of the manorial system, the commutation of feudal dues for money rents, and the change from serf-labour to wage-labour were slow developments. However, there was no further attempt to impose the unpopular Poll Tax until the reign of Henry VIII (1513). The last one to be imposed was in 1698.[20]

The most tragic result of the Peasants' Revolt was the destruction of confidence and trust between the King and his people. Ever afterwards he would be blamed as the scapegoat for a gross breach of faith.

III   Plots and Counterplots

King Richard's uncle John of Gaunt, more skilled in diplomacy than in warfare, was in Scotland negotiating a treaty while his Palace of Savoy was being burnt to the ground by the rebels. The Duke of Lancaster wisely refrained from giving the Scots news of the insurrection, for he feared lest his adversaries would seize the opportunity to plan a major raid over the border. Holinshed in his Chronicles relates that a bitter quarrel now broke out between Gaunt and the Earl of Northumberland, formerly friends.

As a great border Chief, Northumberland keenly resented Lancaster's interference in border affairs, jealous as he was of his rights to lordship in Northumberland and adjoining territories. What rankled also with him was King Richard's order forbidding him from taking retaliatory action against Scotland by way of avenging their raids on Cumberland and Westmoreland. He blamed John of Gaunt's influence.

Whether he really believed the rumours floating about the north of England that the Duke of Lancaster had been outlawed and no longer enjoyed the confidence of the King is uncertain. However, Percy, a great feudal landowner, had been given strict instructions during the Peasants' Revolt for the safekeeping of all the towns and castles under his rule. No person was to be allowed access to Northumberland's castles. Unfortunately, Richard had omitted to make one important exception: his uncle, then the King's Lieutenant in Scotland.

Much to his fury on his return from Scotland, when John of Gaunt presented himself and his retinue before the gates of Berwick and Bamborough Castles, he was refused admittance. "How cometh this to passe. Is there in Northumberland a greater sovereign than I am," said the Duke of Lancaster in a voice of thunder to Sir Matthew Redmayne, Northumberland's Deputy Governor. The embarrassed Redmayne could merely plead that he was obeying the Earl's commands, "a principall and sovereigne of all the heads of Northumberland".

For a month John of Gaunt was entertained by the Scots in the Abbey of Holyrood as a welcome guest. Once the Peasants' Revolt was over, Gaunt received official intimation that the King was eager for his return to help him and advise him on State affairs.

During a Council at Berkhamstead, a furious row erupted between Lancaster and Northumberland in Richard's presence. Percy was accused of ingratitude, for he owed much to Gaunt. The King's uncle charged him with disloyalty. "Henry Percy," he complained, "I beleeved not that ye hadde been so greete in England as to close the gates of citie towne or castell agaynst the Duke of Lancaster."[1] Much incensed, Northumberland retorted that the King's grace had sanctioned his action, whereupon Gaunt exclaimed: "I saye ye have acquytted yourself right yvill and the blame and slander ye have brought me to purge in the presence of the Kynge here preent. I cast down my gage (of battle); rayse it an ye dare." Possessing the hot temper of the Percies, Northumberland broke out into hard words. Richard now acted decisively with a wisdom beyond his years, ordering Northumberland's arrest, although it is not absolutely clear who first issued their challenge. He was soon released. Richard reconciled his uncle and the irate Northumberland, but they never fully trusted one another again.

Both noblemen vied for the support of the Londoners. While Northumberland raised a force of his retainers in the City of London, Lancaster encamped several hundred of his followers at Fulham. One of Richard II's most anxious problems throughout his reign was the armed rivalry of his greater baronage. When the rival noblemen sallied forth to what was known as the Parliament House at Westminster, both parties went there armed to the teeth to the great terror of the citizens. Matters came to such a pass that Richard was forced to forbid in the most peremptory way his uncle and the Earl from taking their retainers to Westminster.

Parliament decided in favour of John of Gaunt, for it was wrong to deny him entrance to Bamborough and Berwick Castles when he held the King's Commission as his Lieutenant. So Northumberland was compelled to make abject apologies to Lancaster.

30

However, both noblemen had been contumacious and arrogant. Parliament now cancelled the Royal Charters of manumission, granted under duress by the King during 'the Hurling Time' ('Shouting Time'). Young Richard was constantly irritated by Parliament's criticism of the Court's extravagance.

Richard's two new guardians appointed during November 1381 were men of widely dissimilar temperament. Richard Fitzalan, Earl of Arundel, once much esteemed by the King's grandfather, a nobleman at once insular and unimaginative, arrogant, honest, but tactless. Although he possessed a certain ability in naval warfare, he was completely antipathetic to the boy King. Arundel was aged about thirty-six when appointed. Michael de la Pole was experienced both as a soldier and as a diplomatist, having fought with the Black Prince in the wars against France. Already over fifty in 1382, he was the son of a wealthy Hull merchant, of the Lancastrian party and known for his fidelity to John of Gaunt. Richard II soon formed a high opinion of de la Pole and he became one of the King's most intimate advisers for some years. He married a Suffolk heiress Katharine de Wingfield, daughter of Sir John de Wingfield, a distinguished soldier and friend of the Black Prince, who had died in 1361. The beautiful medieval church of St. John in Wingfield is resplendent with tombs of de la Poles, Earls and later Dukes of Suffolk. One member of the family later married a sister of Edward IV and Richard III. Nearby is Wingfield Castle where they lived. Richard's Minister, Michael de la Pole, does not lie in the Church for he was to die in exile in a foreign land.

At fifteen, King Richard had reached an age when it was considered advisable for him to make a state marriage. In medieval times, marriages were often consummated at fourteen. It was first proposed that Richard should marry Caterina Visconti, a daughter of a noble Milanese family. Sir Simon Burley and Michael de la Pole headed an embassy to Milan to negotiate a marriage, but returning through Germany, they were captured by brigands and soon released. Despite the Visconti eagerness for the match, for they were prepared to offer as dowry an inestimable quantity of gold, nothing came of it. If such a match had taken place, it would have strengthened Italian influence at Richard's Court.

No such dowry formed a part of the successful negotiations

conducted by Sir Simon Burley and Michael de la Pole for a marriage between Richard and Princess Anne, sister of King Wenceslas of Bohemia, and daughter of the Holy Roman Emperor, Charles IV, King of Bohemia. Actually envoys from Prague, to negotiate a possible marriage, had been in London as early as 1380, but the negotiations were interrupted a few months later by the Peasants' Revolt. The Papacy strongly favoured the match, seeking in the complicated maze of medieval diplomacy to detach the House of Luxembourg from its traditional alliance with the House of Valois in France.[2]

Anne of Luxembourg was a year older than Richard, her childhood having been passed in the extremely cultured atmosphere of her father's court at the Palace on the Hradcany in Prague.[3] He had died, however, in 1380. Anne was cosmopolitan in her sympathies rather than purely Bohemian, since members of her family possessed close links with France, for her Aunt Bona had been Queen of France, and Charles IV's first wife had been Blanche of Valois. One of her uncles, Wenzel of Luxembourg, Duke of Brabant, was a poet and gifted patron of men of letters.[4] Despite Anne's lack of dowry, she brought a strong aura of international prestige. England's link with Bohemia would influence the Wyclifite movement for religious reform in England together with the Hussite movement in Bohemia.

Froissart relates that Anne's journey to England towards the end of December 1381 was full of peril. Burley, under-Chamberlain of the royal household, and a warm supporter of the marriage, was again sent ahead, "travelling with a great equipage" to escort the Princess to England. She was sumptuously entertained by her uncle and aunt, the Duke and Duchess of Brabant. Reports were current that the seas between Holland and Calais were swarming with Norman pirates, consequently it was an anxious time for the young girl. Travelling with their mistress from Calais were courtiers from Prague, chaplains, artists and needy Bohemian ladies. Among Anne's ladies was her maid-of-honour (*domicella*), her cousin, a daughter of the Duke of Teschen. She subsequently married Sir Simon Felbrigg, one of Richard's distinguished Knights, his standard-bearer. At Dover Anne had sore need of rest, for she had scarcely set foot on shore when the ship in which she had embarked was rent in pieces by a terrible storm.[5] It is related that she was greeted with reverence and honour by Richard's younger uncle, Thomas of Woodstock in Kent, but the Earl of Buckingham's greeting could hardly have been sincere, for he had earlier proposed that his nephew should espouse his daughter, Richard's first cousin. Not unnaturally, Richard had declined it. Buckingham, from the first, was hostile to the King, despising him for his apparent unwarlike nature and seeking to undermine him.

When Anne and her cavalcade reached Blackheath, she was given a magnificent reception by the Mayor of London, and the Goldsmiths Company, a rich City Guild, arrayed in their most splendid costumes. In Cheapside, a fairy-like castle had been erected with towers spurting fountains of wine. As a reward for his services, Sir Simon Burley was later appointed Constable of Dover and Warden of the Cinque Ports.

On January 14th 1382, Richard and his bride were married in St. Stephen's Chapel of Westminster Palace, to be followed by Anne's crowning by Archbishop Courtenay in Westminster Abbey. She was no beauty, if one is to judge her from her effigy, but her goodness, her kindness of heart and her compassionate nature appealed strongly to Richard. Owing to her pleadings, a few of the lives of those involved in the Peasants' insurrection were spared. For twelve years they were to live very happily together, an ideal marriage, and he was to confide in her all his griefs during the ensuing quarrels with his barons. Indeed, they seemed utterly content with their devotion to one another, even without children. Whether it was Anne or Richard who was responsible for this childless state we can never know. All the same, Anne was maternal from an early age and because of her love for him, wanted to protect him from the barbs of his enemies. It was disastrous, however, for the country that the King never produced an heir. The two women who mattered most to Richard were his wife and mother, who were in his earlier life, an influence for tolerance and reconciliation. Although the people grew to love Anne, there was at first criticism. Walsingham sourly wrote that Anne had to be taken at a cost of £15,000, while Adam of Usk said that she was bought at a high price.

Richard's most intimate friend was a great nobleman, Robert

de Vere, ninth Earl of Oxford, four years older than the King, and present with him in the Tower when the rebels were shouting for Sudbury's head in St. Katharine's Square. De Vere has been dubbed a favourite, a *mignon*, like the effeminate favourites of Henri III of France, or Piers Gaveston, so passionately loved by his great-grand-father, Edward II. Richard, too, was passionate by nature, especially in his friendships, holding a great affection for Oxford, for they shared many interests, a discriminating interest in art, music, an interest in exquisite dress and a love of magnificence. It is somewhat unlikely that there was a homosexual element in their friendship, though Walsingham, always ready to attribute dishonourable motives to both King and nobleman, thought that Richard's infatuation had a disgraceful origin. Froissart cannot be trusted when he writes about De Vere. He confuses his real father, the Eighth Earl Thomas, with his uncle Aubrey,[6] who had behaved so gallantly during the Peasants' Revolt. "He was the son of Earl Aubrey of Oxford," wrote Froissart, "who never had much of a reputation in this country for honour, wisdom, sound judgement or chivalry."

Samuel Taylor Coleridge, the most perceptive of Shakespearean critics, does not charge Richard with any want of personal courage, but mentions rather "an intellectual feminineness". Nobody is entirely male or female and there was much of the female in Richard of Bordeaux's character. Did he really feel the necessity of ever leaning on the breast of others and of reclining on those who were all the while known to be inferiors? The critic writes of Richard "as a man with a wantonness of external show, a feminine friendism, an intensity of woman-like love of those immediately about him, and a mistaking of the delight of being loved by him for a love of him".[7] There is no reason to suppose that Oxford did not return Richard's devotion, though the King made the grave mistake of rewarding him much too handsomely.

There was nothing unusual in the fourteenth century for a leading nobleman to be affianced at the age of ten to a little girl of four. The wife chosen for him was Philippa of the blood royal, younger daughter of Princess Isabella, elder and favourite daughter of Edward III. She had married an important French nobleman, Enguerrand de Coucy, owner of great domains in Picardy. To attach him more closely to England, Edward had conferred on his son-in-

34

law the Earldom of Bedford. Froissart refers to Philippa's mother too kindly "as a good and beautiful lady, of the highest and noblest descent possible", but in reality she was selfish, compulsively extravagant, and pampered from infancy by her father, who paid her debts. One Christmas, he had given her an ermine-trimmed velvet robe, and another for Philippa.[8] King Edward and her namesake Queen Philippa were generous to her, giving her in infancy an elaborate silver service, various cups, salt cellars, 24 dishes and spoons costing altogether £239 18s 3d. The little girl could have had no premonition that her handsome husband would later cause a scandal by his violent attachment to a Bohemian lady in the train of Richard's Queen. Philippa is a shadowy figure, but Robert de Vere is important for a biographer of Richard II.

Like the King, he possessed magnificent taste, owning a bed with its blue hangings embroidered in gold with *fleur-de-lis* and with owls valued at over £65.[9] In his household there were four minstrels but later in 1388, they were becoming outmoded because authors read their own compositions and verses at Court functions. Richard unwisely created him Chamberlain of England, later Marquis of Dublin (1385) and two years later, Duke of Ireland, thus stirring up jealousy in the minds of the barons. Outside Richard's intimate circle of friends, de Vere was very much disliked and never trusted. Yet he must have possessed extraordinary qualities, culture and intelligence to have inspired so much devotion in Richard. When created Marquis of Dublin, he was given custody of the Lordship of Ireland.

The King's intimate friend, Thomas Mowbray, Earl of Nottingham, hailing from an ancient baronial family possessed a strain of royal blood through his grandmother, Margaret Rutherford. He was almost certainly a more subtle character than de Vere, and less loyal to Richard. Two motives prompted him later, temporarily, to desert the King for the Lords Appellant at a time when Richard desperately needed his friends: Mowbray's barely concealed jealousy of de Vere and his marriage to Elizabeth, a daughter of the King's enemy, the Earl of Arundel and formerly the widow of Sir William de Montagne. Richard with his long memory would never fully forgive Mowbray for his disloyalty in 1387.

Sir Simon Burley, Richard's early tutor and now a most trusted adviser, had been loaded with honours, created Governor of Windsor Castle, made Master of the King's Falcons at the Mews, given vast grants of land and a residence in Thames Street by Baynard's Castle.[10] He had already been rewarded with the Garter after his successful mission to Prague. In 1383 he was appointed Constable of Dover and Warden of the Cinque Ports. Anne of Luxembourg was very fond of him, and he enjoyed the favour of Richard's mother and may have been her lover. However, by his overt encouragement of the young King's struggle for absolute power he was to incur the enmity of Richard's uncle Thomas of Woodstock, of Arundel and other leading magnates. Burley became jealous of Arundel when a naval victory (1386) gained him popularity. These personal friendships, the constant intrigues and deep animosities were of tragic importance in the ensuing years.

To understand the domestic politics of the period, we must realize that the Lancastrian party or faction (as it may be more correctly described) was firmly in the saddle during the early 1380s. One of Richard's most able ministers, Michael de la Pole, a highly competent administrator and staunch friend of John of Gaunt's, certainly encouraged his former royal pupil with an exalted conception of his royal prerogative. However, when appointed Chancellor of England on March 13th 1383, he proved in many ways an excellent minister, successfully trimming the expenses of the royal household, and pursuing an enlightened foreign policy. England was in no condition to embark on costly wars, consequently de la Pole's and John of Gaunt's pursuit of temporary truces with France and Scotland in 1383 was the right one. Evidently, there existed a certain sympathy between de la Pole and King Richard, and he was to learn much about foreign affairs from the older man. The Duke of Lancaster remained a powerful personality, but the King did not really trust his uncle in those early days, probably influenced by Robert de Vere, a jealous nobleman.

The faction opposed to the Court party was led by Thomas of Woodstock, the Earl of Arundel and another magnate of less personality, Thomas Beauchamp, Earl of Warwick.

The Earl of Buckingham, youngest son of Edward III and Queen Philippa, born in 1355 at Woodstock, is a difficult, enigmatic character, fiery, restless, forever dissatisfied, dangerous and treacherous. His chief ally was Arundel, the most vindictive of the King's enemies. Shakespeare puts into the mouth of the dying John of Gaunt in *Richard II* these words: "My brother Gloucester (Richard later created him Duke), plain, well-meaning soul"[11] - it is a travesty of the truth. Buckingham, intensely ambitious, never really content with his status as a younger son, was a reactionary constantly yearning for the glories of the past and hankering for the England of the Black Prince. His alleged devotion to his elder brother, John of Gaunt, is mainly based on a grave occurrence at Salisbury, in 1384, when a Carmelite monk accused Gaunt of treason. Hearing of this, Buckingham had impulsively hastened to the King, and in his presence drawn his sword, swearing that he would kill anybody who accused Gaunt of treason. However, Buckingham was secretly delighted, towards the end of 1385, when his brother was preparing for his foreign expedition to aid our ancient allies, the Portuguese, thinking that in his absence it would be easier for him to achieve his ambitions.

He was openly contemptuous of Richard, his nephew, as King, complaining of his irresolution, his dependence on unworthy favourites, and his lack of bellicosity towards the hereditary enemy, France. Avaricious by nature, Thomas of Woodstock had the sense to marry a wealthy heiress in 1377, Eleanor de Bohun, daughter of a great noblemen, Humphrey de Bohun, Earl of Hereford and Essex and hereditary Constable of England. To his mortification, however, John of Gaunt cleverly arranged to espouse his elder son Henry to Eleanor's younger sister, Mary, despite Buckingham's attempts to acquire the whole Bohun inheritance by trying to persuade his sister-in-law to enter a Convent.

He had a great number of beautiful things at his favourite home, Pleshy Castle, in Essex. A Plantagenet, he resembled his brother, the Black Prince, and his nephew, King Richard, in his cultured tastes, for he owned a bed embroidered with woodwoses (wild men of the wood) jousting,[12] and an embroidered diptych with the Crucifixion and the Coronation of the Virgin. As he grew older, Thomas of Woodstock became increasingly austere, religious and contemptuous of what he considered the soft and luxurious life at his nephew's Court. Unlike Richard, he did not care for good food, being a man who sat little at dinner and supper. Besides his great vellum bible, illuminated with his own arms, and with the swan badge he had assumed from the de Bohuns, in 1397, he had a valuable library at Pleshy containing eighty-three manuscripts,[13] a large number in those days. Both the young King and his uncle owned many tapestries, for during the 1380s and 1390s they were becoming increasingly fashionable among the nobility. Those possessed by Richard depicted the story of St. Edward the Confessor, Charlemagne, Sir Perceval, Octavian of Rome. The subjects of other tapestries in the royal collection were tournaments and courtly scenes.

His marriage to Anne of Luxembourg was influential and beneficial in providing close links between England and Northern and Central Europe. Bohemia in the fourteenth century was an artistic centre, excelling in the art of illumination. It is more than possible that *The Liber Regalis*, the Westminster manuscript on the Coronation rights, in its brilliant colours, now kept in the Muniment Room of Westminster Abbey, owes something to Bohemian artists in the Queen's service. There is a spontaneous delight in colour, gold backgrounds and deep ultramarine blues, characteristic of Bohemian art rather than of English art.[14] Again, in the great missal of Westminster commissioned by Abbot Littlington (painted in 1383 or 1384), a marked Italian influence has been discovered in the crowded crucifixion scene.

Unfortunately, we do not know the names of any Bohemian artists in Queen Anne's retinue accompanying her to England during December 1381. There were priests, Henry of Reybutz, Jacobus, her Confessor, two Knights Johannes Lantgraf and Henricus Potus, and among her ladies, the fascinating and seductive Agnes Launcekron already mentioned. Although people only occasionally said a bad word about Anne, her Bohemian entourage was very unpopular and even accused of rapacity in Parliament. So, many of them were sent home.[15] Since Richard II was interested in horses, he made use of his wife's Bohemians, Rockaus, Walter and John Swartes and Sitbellius, sending them on a mission to Prague to improve his stud.

How far the development of the religious movement in Bohemia and its reformation were influenced by the Wyclifite teachings in England is hard to say. Certainly Hus the Bohemian reformer was familiar with the philosophical works of Wyclif. One German historian Constantin Höfler in a learned article on Anne of Bohemia (written in 1871) stresses the importance of the negotiations for the marriage of Anne and Richard as a factor in the religious development of Bohemia.[16] However, Anne's mother-in-law, Princess Joan, may have influenced her in favour of Wyclif, who died in 1384. Richard remained an orthodox Catholic.

He was no physical weakling. On one occasion during 1383 he rode all night, by relays, from London to Daventry, showing that he possessed much stamina and endurance. Nor did he lack bravery. Numerous references to his courage can be found in the contemporary chronicles, his bravery at Smithfield and Mile End, his stubborn boldness when confronting the rebellious Lords Appellant, and again in his dire extremity at Conway Castle in North Wales when he agreed to the hazardous journey over the wild, mountain passes to Flint where he fell into Henry Bolingbroke's clutches. Three times he led his army in the field, but he only jousted on one occasion, unlike his cousin Henry, whose skill and valour in the jousts held at Smithfield in 1386 endeared him to the citizens. It was a dangerous sport, sometimes resulting in death or injury when a man was violently thrown from his horse. Since his father and grandfather had been frequent jousters, it is, perhaps, curious that Richard refrained from doing so. It is possible that his lofty conception of Kingship was responsible for it, since he might have felt it unkingly to be dehorsed.[17] He mainly presided at tournaments, rarely taking part in them.

The King's upbringing had been lonely. He had no sister, and his elder brother Edward had died almost in infancy, so he depended mainly on his mother, and his wife Anne's love and sympathy. Robert de Vere was his dearest friend, while Burley remained a staunch supporter. Gradually, Anne built up in her Richard the self-confidence and constancy of purpose he sorely needed in dealing with contumacious barons.

One of Richard's worst faults were the terrible Plantagenet rages that sometimes afflicted him, but his wife, so long as she lived, knew how to restrain them. If Richard had a violent temper - and there are too frequent references to them in the Chronicles for one to doubt it - his own great-great grandfather, the warrior King Edward I, 'Hammer of the Scots', was sometimes subject to them. In Edward's wardrobe book (1296-1297), there is this significant entry:

> To Adam the King's goldsmith for a great ruby and a great emerald brought to set in a certain coronet of the Countess of Holland, the King's daughter, in place of the two stones which were lost when the King threw the coronet in the fire at Ipswich.

The reason for Richard's outbursts was his frustration and inability to assume real kingship because factions among the barons were determined to prevent it. The Monk of Westminster mentions the Parliament held at Salisbury from April 29th to May 27th 1384. At first, proceedings were peaceful enough. Members made grateful references to John of Gaunt's efforts to achieve peace in France and Scotland. Then the Earl of Arundel, whose enormous wealth was to some extent derived from the export of wool and from his vast estates, made a tactless and furious attack on the King and government. Arundel's carping criticisms maddened Richard.

> White with passion . . . the King scowled at the Earl. "If it is to my charge that you would lay this, and it is supposed to be my fault that there is misgovernment in the Kingdom, you lie in your teeth. Go to the Devil."[18]

An unearthly silence prevailed. None dared to speak. Then the Duke of Lancaster tactfully intervened, but he gave the impression that he was excusing Arundel to the King. Richard was on rather bad terms with his uncle at the time, finding him overbearing and resenting his advice.

Richard's passionate temper might have been his undoing in another extremely serious episode during the Salisbury Parliament. The King was closeted with Robert de Vere when a Carmelite Friar whose name was John Latemar was ushered in to reveal an alleged crafty and treasonable plot against his life on the part of

John of Gaunt. Instead of calmly inquiring into the accusation, the enraged King immediately ordered his uncle to be put to death, but the surrounding nobles restrained him, saying that it was wrong for anybody to be condemned without trial. When Richard's calm had been restored, he commanded the friar to put his accusation in writing and to name his witnesses. It is often alleged that Richard in his passion threw his cap and shoes out of the window, but it is not true.[19] Perhaps the friar pretended to be insane.

It so happened that the King was due to attend High Mass in Salisbury Cathedral. When he did not arrive, John of Gaunt suddenly appeared in the King's presence and, to his great surprise, his nephew ordered him to be arrested. According to the Monk of Westminster, Gaunt protested so vigorously against the slur to his reputation that the King was convinced of his innocence. When Richard ordered the friar's immediate execution,[20] Gaunt quite reasonably suggested that the man should reveal the names of the instigators of this affair. After being taken to the prison of Salisbury Cathedral, the friar was subjected to brutal tortures, including slow roasting by the King's half-brother, Sir John Holland, in the presence of Sir John Montague (the King's Seneschal). The wretched man later died from his injuries.

At Oxford on June 20th (1384) another Carmelite friar, who had the courage to state in a sermon that Latemar had been lately "done to death" and martyred at Salisbury, after being condemned to life imprisonment, was afterwards restored to liberty. The Lancastrian Chronicles reveal that Richard "wept for pity" when informed that John Latemar had been tortured. So did John of Gaunt. It is possible that we do not know the whole truth about this affair, but it is probable that de Vere, who detested the Duke of Lancaster, had planned the whole affair. The contemporary accounts are based on the information supplied by an eye witness, Sir John Clanvowe, one of the King's Chamber Knights.

It seems that Richard and his uncle differed as to the policy to pursue on political matters at this period. The King and the Court party advocated a preliminary campaign against the marauding Scots, while Gaunt favoured an expedition against France. There was a further plot against the King's uncle in late 1384 in which Robert de Vere and Mowbray were involved. Violence was certainly contemplated, though no evidence exists that the King was privy to the plot. It is likely that John of Gaunt received prior warnings because he wisely absented himself from a Council at Waltham during February 1385. However, the Monk of Westminster relates that Gaunt, wearing a breast-plate under his clothes and escorted by an armed guard went to the Palace of Sheen to confront his nephew. He now upbraided him most severely, telling him it was shameful to keep such counsellors about him for so long, and disgraceful for a King in his own kingdom to avenge himself by a private murder when he was himself above the law. Richard gave his uncle "mild and soothing language", but it was the Princess of Wales who reconciled her son with Gaunt, undertaking a tiring journey to accompany her brother-in-law to visit her son. Always the peacemaker, she used her influence to persuade the Duke of Lancaster to drop his resentment against de Vere and Mowbray.

Adam of Usk's story of Princess Joan's arduous journey by night from Wallingford to London during 1387 must be untrue because the King's mother had died in late 1385. On this occasion the Chronicler makes her say:[21]

> At thy coronation, my son, I rejoiced that it had fallen to my lot to be the mother of an anointed King; but now I grieve, for I foresee the fall which threatens thee, the work of accursed flatterers.

It is easy to condemn him for listening too readily to the blandishments of favourites, but he was only seventeen.

Richard's relations with his Archbishop of Canterbury, William Courtenay, son of Hugh Earl of Devon, and a former Bishop of Hereford and London, were very poor. Although Courtenay had earlier quarrelled with John of Gaunt, resentful that he supported John Wyclif, he was critical also of the King's conduct. One day after Richard had been dining with one of his City friends, Sir Nicholas Brembre, he entered his barge on the Thames. Off Westminster he encountered by chance the Archbishop accompanied by the Earl of Buckingham, Richard's youngest uncle. High words passed between the King and Courtenay.

42

Richard drew his sword, and would have run the Archbishop through on the spot if he had not been stoutly resisted by Buckingham, Sir John Devereux, a distinguished soldier and diplomat, and Sir Thomas Trivet, a Knight of the Chamber.[22]

There was excessive heat that summer (1385) lasting from the beginning of May until the nativity of the Virgin, September 5th.

Across the Channel during that summer, Charles VI of France was planning an invasion of England, which was ill prepared to resist it. One army was to attack from the Flemish base of Sluys, while a renowned soldier named Sir Jean de Vienne was to land in Scotland with an army of 2,000 to join in an attack on the English. However, the French invasion from the Low Countries never materialized.

Richard was no soldier and this was his first experience of a military campaign. The customary quarrels occurred between rival baronial factions. At Beverley Minster in Yorkshire, a serious dispute erupted between two squires in the service of Sir John Holland, the King's half-brother, and two of the Earl of Stafford's grooms, in the course of which Holland's two squires were slain. He at once complained to the King, having learnt that the Earl's retainers had found sanctuary. Richard, always keen to respect the rights of sanctuary, forbade his half-brother to break it, promising him that he would so arrange matters that it would "conduct to his interests and honour alike".[23] Unfortunately, Holland happened to meet Ralph, the son and heir of Hugh, Second Earl of Stafford, on the way to York and, hot-tempered by nature, avenged his murdered squires by killing him. It was a rash act, putting Holland entirely in the wrong. The Earl of Stafford, grievously mourning the loss of his heir, asked Richard for justice against his son's murderer, otherwise he and his retainers would take the law into their own hands.

The King's decision to banish his half-brother from the realm and confiscate his goods was entirely justified in the circumstances. According to the Monk of Westminster, Richard was extremely upset, abandoning himself for some time to tears. It was a painful decision, not made easier by his mother Princess Joan's tearful pleas on behalf of her son by her first marriage. It is said that her great distress hastened her own death that summer. Richard's mother, so tender by nature, died on August 8th at Wallingford, troubled by the ever mounting violence in her son's kingdom. The King mourned for her and was the poorer for her loss, for she had been a wise mediator in his quarrels with his uncles. Only his beloved Anne remained to use her beneficial influence for peace and restraint.

On August 6th, Richard with his army moved on across the border for the invasion of Scotland. How wasteful this intermittent warfare with Scotland seems to us today, but in the late fourteenth century, the English considered many of the Scots savages, while the latter hated the English.

It is difficult to conceive that Richard at eighteen, so urbane, would have ordered the wanton destruction of the Abbeys of Melrose and Newbottle or the sacking of Edinburgh and the Abbey of Holyrood. His uncle protested, perhaps influenced by his hospitable reception in Scotland four years before.

It was now that the King, always ready throughout his reign to bestow titles, created his uncle Edmund of Langley, Earl of Cambridge, Duke of York, while Thomas of Woodstock, Earl of Buckingham, became Duke of Gloucester. Michael de la Pole was rewarded with an earldom, that of Suffolk.

Froissart dismisses Edmund of Langley as lacking in ambition and initiative; he was rather indolent and mainly concerned with his pleasures. All the same, he was a more pleasant character than his brother, now Duke of Gloucester. He tried to save Sir Simon Burley's life when condemned by the Lords Appellant. Coleridge considers that in Shakespeare's *Richard II*, York's character is admirably drawn, "his religious loyalty struggling with a deep grief and indignation at the King's follies".[24] He was in fact a man of good intentions but feeble deeds. The Monk of Westminster is mistaken when he mentions that Edmund was created Duke of Canterbury, though it is possible that the title was first bestowed on him and later changed.

John of Gaunt's men-at-arms and archers formed a powerful component of Richard's army, but he was soon at loggerheads with his nephew on matters of strategy. He favoured overrunning the West Lowlands as the most effective means of opposing the

44

invasion of the Scots over the English border whereas Richard considered that the risks involved in invading territory bare of supplies did not justify this project. It was, however, unwise of him to annoy John of Gaunt by saying: "You and your Lords may live upon your private stores, but the common soldier perishes by the way. I will not push into these wilds to destroy my army."[25] Richard erred in alienating his uncle when he most needed his support in the imminent crisis with his barons. Any chance of a real reconciliation between the two was thwarted by de Vere's constant jibes at Gaunt. He even hinted that the Duke of Lancaster secretly hoped that his nephew would be killed in the wild moorlands of Scotland. When the King decided on the withdrawal of his army through Berwick, Gaunt acquiesced. Little had been accomplished except to deter the French from using Scotland as their base for many years.

It was now that young Harry Percy, aged nineteen, was acquiring his remarkable reputation for bravery, the terror of the Scots and the French alike. He was a legend in his own day, like the Black Prince. We admire him for his heroic qualities, though the historical Percy differed in several ways from Shakespeare's magnificent portrait.[26] He had a touch of cruelty, as he later showed at Homildon, and he was superstitious like most people in medieval times. He never forgot that a soothsayer in his own Northumberland had once predicted that he would meet his end at Berwick, naturally jumping to the conclusion that the Berwick on the border was intended, not a village near Shrewsbury. After the Scots and the French attacked Carlisle on September 7th, being forced to retreat, Hotspur fell upon them by night, killing many of them and taking others prisoner. Holinshed in his *Chronicles of Scotland* relates that he acquired the name "from his so often pricking as one that seldom time rested when there was any service to be done about". His enemies, the French and the Scots, called him Harre Hotesporre. "While others were unoccupied or in quiet sleep, he laboured unwearied, as if his spur was hot, which we called Hotesporre." He acquired a European reputation, though he was no strategist. At Richard's Court, Harry Percy was held up as an example to aspiring courtiers, a model of chivalry:

And by his light
Did all the chivalry of England move
To do brave acts.[27]

Percy possessed one curious trait. He stammered when excited, and it was the fashion among the courtiers to imitate this stammer. Richard also had a hesitation in his speech. The King's own favourite among the Percies, who were to reach the height of their influence towards the end of the century, was Sir Thomas, Hotspur's worldly, urbane, uncle, a man with military, naval and diplomatic experience. He was soon to receive an important appointment at Richard's Court.

In the King's Court circle, Sir Simon Burley was a powerful influence, holding the offices of Vice-Chamberlain and Castellan of Windsor. With the help of Sir Baldwin Raddington, later Constable of the Wardrobe, a loyal and efficient servant of Richard II, he was responsible for organizing the Chamber Knights and squires into a competent, royal bodyguard. Close to Richard also were Richard Medford, Clerk of the King's Chapel and later Bishop of Chichester and Salisbury, and John Bacon, his Secretary.

Richard's love of jewelry and of exotic dress were marked features of his character. He wore a dress of white satin, embroidered with leeches, water rocks, hung with fifteen silver-gilt mussels and fifteen cockles of white silver trees, the doublet embroidered with gold orange trees. For his finery in dress the King was much criticized: it is amusing to record that the King invented the linen handkerchief for his own personal use, as described in the Wardrobe accounts.[28]

Richard's Queen introduced one important new fashion into England, the side-saddle, a kind of bench with a hanging step where both feet were set. This style of riding needed a squire to hold the rein of a lady's horse and was used chiefly in processions.[29]

Anne of Luxembourg shared her Richard's love of the theatre, spectacular show and pageantry, and his taste for hot baths. However, she possessed more serious interests. She could read and write in English, Latin and German, and she owned a bible written in Bohemian, German and Latin. Thomas Arundel, Bishop of Ely and later Archbishop of Canterbury, a younger brother of the Earl of Arundel, never well disposed towards Richard, said that "in the reading of godly books she was more diligent than are the prelates themselves". Stow, in his *Survey of London*, says that she introduced into England one disagreeable fashion: 'piked shoes tied to their knees with silken laces or chains of silver and gilt'.

IV   Rebellion

While Richard was still in Scotland, the Portuguese under João I (John I) on August 14th 1385 gained a great victory over Juan I (John of Transmare) and the Castilians at the Battle of Aljubarrota, an important date in Portuguese history whereby that gallant little nation acquired their national independence. In their army were many English volunteers, proud to take part in this decisive battle. The Monk of Westminster relates that the flower of the Spanish nobility were killed - about 7,500 men - but there was one traitor in their ranks named Lopo Gomez de Lira.

Throughout these years, the Duke of Lancaster had never relinquished his real ambition through his second wife Constanza of Castile to be King of Castile, and it seemed now that circumstances favoured the preparation of an expedition to Spain and Portugal. The diplomacy of Pope Urban V in Rome supported the King's uncle, for he was eager to organize a coalition against his hated rival in Avignon, Clement VII, the friend of France.

Richard, only too ready to get rid of his tiresome uncle, gave him a personal loan of £13,000, while Lombard and London Merchants advanced money for the expedition. Little did the King realize the imminent dangers that were to engulf him during John of Gaunt's absence from the kingdom. Another uncle, the Duke of Gloucester, a far more sinister personality than Gaunt, was preparing a hornet's nest for his despised nephew.

During the autumn session (1385) Parliament agreed to financing an expedition to Portugal, and to provide funds for the relief of Ghent, although unaware that that town had already fallen into French hands. What angered the King, however, was Parliament's insistence that he should publish the names of his ministers for the coming year and that he should submit his accounts for the inspection of a parliamentary commission. Richard, always jealous of his royal prerogatives, demurred, saying he would be his own master, nor would he agree to submit his accounts.

It was a lovely sight, that July day (July 7th 1386), as Gaunt's Lancastrian fleet embarked from Plymouth. Holinshed described the scene. "The seas were calm, the aire sweet and the winds pleasant and agreable", while Froissart wrote: "It was a great hearte to see the galleys glyde on the sea approaching the lande full of men-of-armes and archers, seeking for some adventures." An enormous army accompanied the expedition, tailors, goldsmiths, craftsmen, chaplains, cooks, scullions and ministrels.[1] Among John of Gaunt's entourage was the King's tempestuous half-brother John Holland, who had fallen violently in love with the Duke of Lancaster's daughter Elizabeth, and married her. Now Richard pardoned him his crime of violence provided he should accompany John of Gaunt's expedition.

The Duke of Lancaster met the King of Portugal for the first time at the Ponte de Mouro on the Minho border. Escorted by Sir Thomas Percy, Gaunt's elder daughter, Philippa, travelled to Oporto. There on St. Valentine's Day (February 14th 1387), Philippa, together with John I, wearing cloth of gold and golden crowns, rode on white horses to the Cathedral, to be married. The future mother of that great Portuguese Prince 'Henry the Navigator' had been brought up very strictly in her father's resplendent palace of the Savoy. In Portugal she insisted that a hundred couples whom she discovered living in open sin get married immediately. Provided he was suitably rewarded, John of Gaunt was willing to relinquish his own ambitions, happy that his two daughters by Blanche of Lancaster would become Queens. He himself surrendered his claims to the throne of Castile after reaching an agreement with the King of Spain to pay him large sums in gold. At Windsor, the Portuguese envoys drew up a new treaty in which the English guaranteed their support for the new King of Portugal against any attempt from Castile to take over his throne. A clause in the treaty provided that ten large Portuguese galleys were for the special use of Richard II for six months, at the expense of the Portuguese Treasury. Portugal is now our most ancient ally for over six hundred years.

It was folly on the part of the King, when his relations with Parliament were already strained, to antagonize them further by raising Robert de Vere to the first Marquisate in English history. He was seated in Parliament above the Earls. To their great annoyance, de Vere was given not only palatine rights over the Irish Pale, but an annual income of 5,000 marks from Irish revenues paid by the English Exchequer. It seemed a deliberate act of defiance, raising the comparatively inexperienced nobleman to such high honours. A formidable faction of the opposition to the Court party, including the Earl of Arundel, the Duke of Gloucester, the Bishop of Ely, the Earl of Warwick and their new recruit, Thomas Mowbray, who for the time being had deserted the King because of his jealousy of de Vere, showed their anger. Yet they were quite wrong to condemn Sir Simon Burley and the new Earl of Suffolk as unworthy favourites. Both Burley and de la Pole were, in fact, men of outstanding ability. Moreover, the unscrupulous barons - ambitious, self-seeking, greedy, and hypocritical in their claim to be acting for the welfare of the Kingdom - were very much to blame. The young King needed their understanding and sympathy, instead of which he got Gloucester's and Arundel's constant criticism and hostility.

Gordon Daviot (a pseudonym of a female dramatist), in his fine play *Richard of Bordeaux* (1932), puts into the mouth of Michael de la Pole words entirely fitting to his character. In a scene when various counsellors are present, he says:

> Not one of us has walked alone into a hostile mob and quelled it, as the King did . . . A mob which had just seen their leader killed before their eyes. That was a thing done without prompting out of his own spirit. The whole future of this country depended upon a boy of fifteen and only his courage and initiative saved it from chaos. There is wonderful mettle there, my Lords. It is for us merely to guide it, as Sir Simon Burley suggests, and not to thwart and deny it.[2]

That was the source of Richard's tragedy, the refusal of a decadent baronage to see his merits.

The young King possessed influential friends in the City of London, but he was no longer 'the Londoners' King'. A powerful element now opposed him. The governing body of the City was composed of members of the merchant capitalist class throughout his reign. Ruth Bird in *The Turbulent London of Richard II* depicts the constant lawlessness in the capital, the feuds between the magnates. On two occasions, Richard's most influential friend Sir Nicholas Brembre had resorted to force to achieve the office of Mayor of London, particularly in the autumn of 1383. Brembre was a strong supporter of Richard's, an immensely wealthy man willing for about ten years to lend vast sums - about £2,970[3] - to the King. Like Walworth, he was a member of the Fishmongers' Guild, and mostly described as a grocer, sometimes as a merchant (*mercator*) and as a "wolmongere". His marriage to Idonia, an heiress, had added to his wealth. He possessed six manors in Kent and three in Middlesex.

Opposed to Brembre was another City personality, John de Northampton, also a man of considerable wealth and property, acquired partly through his marriage. Northampton, when he attained the office of Mayor, pursued policies favouring the poor, aiming to prevent them being forced to offer more than they could afford at baptisms, marriages and requiems. Whenever possible he attacked dishonest fishmongers, for he genuinely wished to lower the price of food. Under his mayoralty, a man John Welburgham, was convicted of selling stinking fish.[4] The Mayor ordered the dishonest fishmonger not only to repay the money he had received from the sale of the stinking fish, but also to be exhibited in the stocks to be the object of ridicule of the bystanders. His vigorous campaign against the fishmongers earned him many enemies. He also conducted an energetic campaign against common harlots, ensuring that those who were not only whores but thieves and "molls" should be ordered to don hoods of striped cloth, so that they might easily be identified.

During Richard II's reign, the maintenance of houses for the convenience of prostitutes was always strictly prohibited to within the walls of the City, but there were the licensed houses of Bankside (maintained until the reign of Henry VII, 1485). Stow calls them "stew-houses". Even such a distinguished Mayor of London as William Walworth owned various "stew-houses", for Wat Tyler and the men of Kent took the opportunity to spoil them during the Peasants' Revolt.[5] John of Northampton was quite severe in his attempts to cleanse the City of disorderly women. For instance, in 1385, Elizabeth, wife of Henry Moring, pretending to pursue the craft of brodery, employed a girl called Johanna and others as apprentices. These she encouraged to follow a lewd life, hiring them out to friars and chaplains. When apprehended, she was ordered to be borne through the City on a cart and placed in the stocks with her hair cut off.

Northampton's patron was John of Gaunt. He was almost certainly a follower of Wyclif, a member of the Drapers' Guild opposed to the Victuallers', who enjoyed the King's favour. During his mayoralty, the trial of a man named John Aston, a follower of Wyclif, was violently interrupted by the Londoners showing the strong hold the opinions of the religious reformer had on London. However, John of Northampton's fortunes declined sharply during November 1383 though Richard, strangely enough, had interfered the year before to aid his re-election. On this occasion, Brembre's election to the mayoralty was carried by force and many of Northampton's friends and supporters either killed, imprisoned or exiled. The infuriated drapers now demanded a new poll, tactlessly asking for the help of John of Gaunt. Fierce passions raged in the City, aggravated by Northampton's arrest.

Richard, as President, took part in the proceedings when John of Northampton was tried by the Council at Reading. When he demanded a postponement of his trial until his patron could be present - he was absent in the north - Richard lost his temper, exclaiming: "I will teach you that I am your judge, whether my uncle is absent or not."[6] Eventually, a new trial took place before Chief Justice Tressilian in the Tower when John of Northampton, having been condemned, was consigned to languish imprisoned in Tintagel Castle. There he remained until 1388. Richard's friend, Nicholas Brembre, was again opposed by a draper named Twyford, but force was again resorted to in the mayoral contest, resulting in victory for Brembre. It was unfortunate that an influential majority in the City, now estranged from Richard, later sided with the so-called Lords Appellant during the ensuing troubles. The opposition to King Richard's favourites mounted.

When Nicholas de Littlington, an outstanding abbot and benefactor to Westminster Abbey, died during November, the King required the Prior and Convent to respect his wishes that Brother John Lakingheath should be elected abbot, the possible author of the Monk of *Westminster Chronicle*.[7] He had formerly served as steward of Abbot Littlington's household. The monks, however, by way of compromise chose their own candidate, Brother William Colchester. Later, through the mediation of good friends, Richard became reconciled to the appointment, writing a gracious letter on Colchester's behalf to the Roman Curia, notifying Pope Urban VI of his assent to the election (January 21st 1387).

The mood of the so-called 'Wonderful Parliament' reflecting the feeling in the country generally was deeply apprehensive when it assembled during 1386. Another French invasion was threatened from the Low Countries, but it again never materialized. It gave the Duke of Gloucester and his faction the excuse to pose as the only defenders of the realm, a cunning ruse whereby they disguised their real intentions.

Most of the Lancastrian Chronicles, such as the *Knighton Chronicle*,[8] are hostile to the King and his ministers. He is described as stubbornly, even contemptuously, resisting the attempts of the magnates to rid and cleanse the Kingdom of the corrupt flatterers to whom he was doltishly attached. He is accused of wishing to destroy the lords hostile to the Court party by intimidation, trickery and even a resort to arms. As a contrast to this biased portrayal of Richard's actions and behaviour, the hostile barons are represented as good and patriotic Englishmen, seeking only to promote the welfare of the kingdom. In reality, they were ruthless, ambitious and utterly selfish, ready to throw England into turmoil to achieve their own ends.

Parliament immediately attacked two of Richard's most valued ministers, the Chancellor, the Earl of Suffolk, and the Treasurer, John Fordham, demanding their dismissal and impeachment. *The Knighton Chronicon* accuses de la Pole of corruption, of forcing people to pay him a fine before their suits were settled. Thomas Walsingham in *The Historia Anglicana* charges him with the offence of persuading the young King to farm out the taxes to him and to embezzle the money intended for the Brotherhood of St. Anthony. Richard's constant loyalty to his friends never faltered however. He was to remain true to Burley, Suffolk and de Vere.

Throughout that exasperating autumn, Richard rather than remain in Westminster, chose to stay in one of his favourite palaces, Eltham, near Blackheath. There is an aura of peace about it even today after six hundred years, but how much more lovely it must have been then, with its gardens and deer park. It was a palace much cherished by Plantagenet kings.

When informed of Parliament's demand that Suffolk should be dismissed, Richard said haughtily: "I would not dismiss the meanest (lowliest) of my scullions at Parliament's command."[9] Richard did not lack good judgement in the appointment of his ministers. It is evident that Suffolk had clear ideas of what was meant by sound bureaucratic government resting on the prerogative.[10] However, like Burley, it is possible that he filled the mind of the King with too exalted a conception of it.

The King suggested that the Commons should send to him a deputation of forty of the more experienced members, to Eltham. There existed mutual distrust between King and Parliament. A rumour persisted that it was intended to destroy these delegates either by an armed attack while on their way to confer with Richard or at a banquet, a story probably concocted by Richard Exton, then Mayor of London, an enemy of the King's friend, Sir Nicholas Brembre. Instead, Parliament decided to send the Duke of Gloucester and Thomas Arundel, Bishop of Ely, to confer with Richard. Thomas Arundel was a much more subtle and able prelate than his brother, the tactless and opinionated Earl of Arundel.

We do not know exactly what happened at this historic interview, but there would probably have been the sharp hectoring of his uncle telling his nephew that an ancient statute[11] provided for annual parliaments. If the King, except for illness or other necessary cause, was absent from Parliament for forty days, the members were permitted to disperse. Adam of Usk's contemporary account is confused at this juncture and is of no value whatsoever. The King replied angrily that he was well aware that the Lords and Commons intended to resist his wishes. In these circumstances he thought it wise to seek aid against his opponents from Charles VI, the King of France. He preferred this course rather than to yield to his own subjects.

Then the venomous Gloucester could not resist reminding his nephew of the fate of his ancestor Edward II, deposed and later murdered in Berkeley Castle. According to Knighton, the two lords made impassioned appeal to Richard's reason and patriotism, arguing that the King of France was the deadly enemy of the realm. If Charles were to set foot in England, he would deprive Richard of his throne rather than bring him aid. Knighton quotes Gloucester's and the Bishop of Ely's words:

> If the King from bad counsel of any sort or from stupid obstinacy . . . or from a singularly rash will . . . shall alienate himself from his people and shall wish not to be governed . . . by the laws of the kingdom . . . but shall wish arbitrary in his own mad counsels to exercise his own personal will obstinately, it is permitted then with common agreement with the Consent of the people of the realm to depose the King himself from his royal throne, and to set . . . in his place someone quite nearly related from the royal house.

It seems more than possible that Gloucester aimed at the throne, though his elder brother, John of Gaunt, at the time in the Iberian Peninsula, had the better right. Actually, Richard's presumptive heir was Roger Mortimer, Fourth Earl of March, directly descended from Edward III's third son Lionel, Duke of Clarence, a genial giant of a man, who had died in 1368.

Richard was forced to submit to the Lords' wishes. On October 23rd, Suffolk was dismissed from his post at Chancellor, while the astute Thomas Arundel took his place. Bishop John Gilbert and John Waltham, both of the Gloucester faction, became Treasurer and Keeper of the Privy Seal. To Richard's mortification, he was deprived of his friends. Suffolk was impeached by his enemies, though the King made desperate attempts to save him. One friend, Sir William Scrope of Bolton, made an impassioned speech in Parliament on de la Pole's behalf, reminding members of his distinguished thirty years' service to the State. Despite the attempts to accuse Suffolk of treason - an absurd charge - his enemies could only frame an unconvincing case for peculation. According to one authority,[12] the impeachment degenerated into three trivial charges, behind which motives of malice or private interest may be suspected.[13] Suffolk was ordered to be imprisoned in Windsor Castle and deprived of his properties. The young King continued to defy Parliament, boldly extending a generous invitation to de la Pole to be his guest during the Christmas festivities at Windsor, and temporarily remitting his forfeitures.

One minor official, Geoffrey Chaucer, lost his post as Controller of the London Wool Custom in the 'Wonderful Parliament' ending in November 1386. When in session, Parliament had incessantly clamoured for the banishment of Robert de Vere, Marquis of Dublin, but Richard had paid not the slightest heed to their wishes. To have created him Duke of Ireland was extreme folly on the part of the King, antagonizing the opposition party even more. De Vere, one of the King's and Queen's most intimate circle, had fallen deeply in love with Agnes Launcekron, one of Queen Anne's Bohemian ladies. He even wanted to divorce his wife Philippa, much to the anger of the royal dukes, who resented the insult more because Philippa possessed royal blood, rather than for any moral consideration.

Froissart was especially critical of de Vere, probably because of his friendship with Philippa's father, the Sieur de Coucy, saying that his treatment of his wife was "the principal thing that took away his honour". It was said of Richard that he was too hypnotized by his favourite to do other than assist in his own cousin Phillipa's repudiation. Even the nobleman's mother showed her disapproval by taking the lady to live with her. Divorce was by no means infrequent in that age, particularly if one had influential friends. When Robert submitted his appeal to Rome, Richard begged Pope Urban VI for favourable consideration, knowing of Robert's infatuation for the fascinating Agnes and that he wanted to marry her.

Whilst in session, the 'Wonderful Parliament' had appointed fourteen Commissioners, entrusted with the authority to amend the administration. They were now fully in control of the Exchequer, and the Great and Privy Seals, but a gleam of hope remained for Richard. Their powers were granted only for twelve months. For the time being he was stripped of power. He naturally resented the appointment of the Commissioners, being compelled to submit. At the same time he protested that no law, sanctioned during the Parliament, had altered 'Sa Prérogatif et les Libertées de sa dite Corone'.[14] The Commissioners included the Archbishops of Canterbury and York (Alexander Neville, a friend of the King).

the Dukes of York and Gloucester, the Bishops of Winchester and Exeter, the Abbot of Waltham, the Earl of Arundel and his brother, the Bishop of Ely, among others.[15]

On March 12th 1387, the Monk of Westminster relates that "a wonderful stroke of luck came in answer to our prayers". The Earl of Arundel, in the naval battle of Cadzand taking place off the Kent coast at Margate, succeeded in capturing a hundred ships from La Rochelle laden with wine destined for Sluys. The booty amounted to more than 8,000 tuns of wine. The Londoners were delighted when much of the precious wine was distributed free to them, the rest being distributed and sold all over England at 4d per gallon, a popular gesture guaranteeing the backing of the Londoners.

During that Christmas at Windsor, Richard, now in his twentieth year, conferred anxiously with the Duke of Ireland and the Earl of Suffolk, sounding them as to his best course of action. Deprived of his Seals, the King had no authority to raise a proper army, though for the first time the Chronicles mention the King's bodyguard of Cheshire archers and Welsh pikemen. It is probable that it was Michael de la Pole who advised Richard to sound the judiciary as to the legality of the Commission set up by Parliament. During the spring and summer (1387) Richard went on an extended progress to York, Lancashire, Cheshire and North Wales. Firstly, the Court moved to Shrewsbury, a town familiar to Richard II. At Shrewsbury and later at Nottingham, five legal luminaries including the five Chief Justices, Tressilian, Belknap, Holt, Burgh and Cary, Chief Baron of the Exchequer, when asked various questions by the Sergeants-at-law, gave it as their opinion that the Commission was unlawful as infringing upon the royal prerogative.[16] They adjudged that those who had procured it had rendered themselves liable to the penalties of treason. The direction of procedure in Parliament and the power to dissolve it was a matter for the King, and the Commons could not impeach Crown officers without the royal consent. Consequently, the impeachment and condemnation of the Earl of Suffolk was irregular and revocable.

It is easy for those hostile to the King and to the Court party to declare that these legal opinions were obtained under duress, but it is hardly fair to Richard. He gave the judges at least a week to think over their answers. It was only later that these same judges, fearing for their lives during the Merciless Parliament (1388) pleaded that they had given their opinions under duress.

Edward III had allowed the great barons to raise private armies for the purpose of fighting abroad. Despite various attempts to curtail them, the barons had maintained these men in their pay and livery, so that they not only became a danger to the peace of the realm, but a constant menace to the throne. Consequently, it gave Richard the impulse to organize a private royal army in his own pay and livery. While on his progress, his officers were busy enlisting men and distributing royal liveries of red and white with crowns of gold and badges of the white hart, the emblem of the King.[17] Richard was Earl of Chester, and he derived much encouragement and support from Cheshire and North Wales. Many of the Black Prince's best archers came from the forest of Macclesfield.

It was during September that Richard appointed the Duke of Ireland Justiciar of Chester and North Wales. By now de Vere had married his mistress Agnes Launcekron, living in great splendour with her at Chester, as his inventories later brought to London show. Among the articles inventoried are two saddles for *demoiselles* of Bohemia and one old saddle of the Bohemian fashion.

What a misfortune for Richard that his secret dealings with the judges had been leaked to the Duke of Gloucester by the Archbishop of Dublin, one of the witnesses. It greatly alarmed the King's uncle and his confederates that the judges had interpreted the law of treason more widely than the narrow definition of the Statute of 1352 when Edward III had expressly excluded from the act of treason the offence "of accroaching on the King's powers" (or prerogative). Yet before 1352 it had constituted the crime of treason with all its penalties. To be adjudged a traitor in the fourteenth century entailed for a condemned man the awful punishment of half-hanging, disembowelling while still alive, then beheading and quartering the remains. If Gloucester and his friends were to fall into Richard's hands, they had no illusions that they might be tried and condemned for treason.

There is no doubt that Richard miscalculated the extent of his power when returning to Westminster at the end of October. At first the citizens of London seemed to give him their support, but in reality, Gloucester controlled the capital, backed up by the feudal levies of Arundel and Warwick. According to the Monk of Westminster, the King made a ceremonial entry into the city on November 10th when the Mayor and chief citizens came out to meet him, dressed in the royal livery of white and red. So they rode ahead of him in procession through the City as far as Charing Mews where Richard removed his shoes. Attended by the Archbishop of York, and the Earl of Suffolk, barefooted like himself, he went to the Church of St. Peter (Westminster Abbey). Once again in a crisis, Richard found consolation in prayer.

Three days later, the King summoned Gloucester, Arundel and Warwick to his counsel, but the rebellious lords had already assembled their archers and men-at-arms in Harringay Forest, Middlesex, each man wearing the badge of his lord, Gloucester's Swan, Arundel's horse and Warwick's bear. Then this formidable private army moved on to Waltham Forest in open defiance of King Richard. When refusing to attend him in Council, they alleged that they had archenemies at Richard's elbow and dared not approach him.

Thomas de Beauchamp, Earl of Warwick, was of the ancient nobility, aged about forty-three, a soldier, who had held high command in France under John of Gaunt and Edmund of Langley during the reign of Richard's grandfather. He was a less aggressive character than Gloucester or Arundel. Marie Louise Bruce in her biography, *The Usurper King*, says that Warwick is best known for Guy's Tower, an addition to that lovely Warwick Castle, so picturesquely set on the Avon, probably commemorating his mythical ancestor, Guy of Warwick. The three noblemen bitterly resented the new men at Richard's Court.

On November 14th, they published an 'appeal of treason' against the King's friends, Robert de Vere, Duke of Ireland, the Earl of Suffolk, Archbishop Neville, Chief Justice Tressilian and Sir Nicholas Brembre, a former Mayor of London. To gain time, Richard decided to refer the matter to Parliament. His real purpose was to give Neville and Suffolk the opportunity to escape abroad. Meanwhile, de Vere was still in Cheshire, organizing an army to rescue the King from his enemies.

On November 17th, seated in the hall of Westminster Palace, the King looked on as the three lords appellant made a dramatic entrance, their arms linked together, and clad in cloth of gold.[18] They entered the hall in chain mail, attended by armed followers, making a low obeisance three times before Richard. The lords, when making their 'appeal of treason' against the King's friends, were careful to stress their own loyalty, feigned though it was, "making us eager to move as quickly as possible against those creatures so that we can save ourselves - indeed the entire kingdom - from treachery lurking unseen and the snares that spell death".[19]

News now arrived that de Vere was marching with his army to support the King from Chester towards the Severn Valley. It was civil war. On hearing this, Richard's first cousin, Henry of Derby, and Thomas Mowbray, Earl of Nottingham, the King's former intimate friend, openly took the plunge and joined the rebel lords. Both were enemies of de Vere. Henry Bolingbroke (so named because of his birth at Bolingbroke in Lincolnshire) resented the Duke of Ireland all the more because of his intrigues against his father.

From boyhood there had been a mutual jealousy, a deep-rooted suspicion and distrust between Richard and Henry. They were too dissimilar in temperament. Richard, an artist by temperament, perceptive, delighting in beautiful things, a superb patron of writers, artists and architects, a lover of exquisite cooking, and revealing a real gift for kingship when given the chance. He was certainly not without talents for the external show of monarchy. The actor in him constantly needed self-dramatization. On the other hand, the wary, politically minded, calculating Bolingbroke, was an extrovert excelling in field sports and jousting, as well as being cultured and well educated. Yet despite his extensive travels later, in Prussia, Lithuania and Jerusalem - he was far more travelled than Richard - Henry never revealed any real understanding of other nations, as exemplified in his contemptuous reference to the Welsh after he became Henry IV and was about to embark on the wars in Wales. "What care we for these barefooted scrubs?" This hardly showed him in a favourable light. Richard, however, showed real understanding of the Irish problem later in 1394 and a feeling for the Irish. Henry was red-haired, athletic, stockier in build than his cousin and less tall, and he possessed a great love and knowledge of music.[20] It is curious to think of them both in boyhood, being knighted in St. George's Chapel, Windsor Castle, and receiving from their benign, old grandfather Edward III, the insignia of the Order of the Garter. Each then swore, taking a sacred oath, repeated in their treble voices (Richard was ten, his cousin eleven) that he would not bear arms against his companion, unless in the war of his liege lord, or in his own justice. Perhaps some boyish recollection of a solemn oath had so far restrained Henry from betraying his loyalty to the monarchy which had been ingrained in him by his father. Warily watching on the sidelines, he was now openly to side against Richard.

The three Lords Appellant eagerly welcomed Henry, Earl of Derby to their ranks, appointing him commander to their army. Neither Bolingbroke nor de Vere had any experience in warfare, but Henry proved the better soldier. Yet Robert did not lack courage, for apart from Brembre, who openly campaigned for Richard in London, he was the only one of the King's partisans to show fight against the rebel lords.

There are several contemporary accounts of the Campaign of Radcot Bridge, December 1387, firstly the so-called 'Malvern', the continuation of Higden's *Polychronicon*. The writer was a monk of Westminster basing his account on the direct evidence of members of the Appellants' army who, immediately after the battle, marched straight to London, remaining in the vicinity of Westminster during the following six months of the 'Merciless Parliament'. A more valuable account is that of the continuator of Knighton, a contemporary canon of St. Mary's Leicester, though it may be biased. This writer used the evidence of a Leicester dependant of John of Gaunt. He was actually serving under his son, the Earl of Derby, on the Upper Thames during the campaign.

J.N.L. Myres in a detailed article[21] assesses the merits of the various accounts. It seems probable that de Vere together with Sir Thomas Molyneux, Constable of Chester, Sir Ralph Vernon and Sir Ralph Ratcliffe, with about 4,000 to 5,000 men intended to move from Chester to London only to hear that the rebel lords were blocking their path at Northampton. Forced to make a diversion, de Vere and his men marched to Stow-on-the-Wold. Meanwhile, the lords, by their cunning strategy, completely outwitted the Duke of Ireland. While the Earl of Derby with his forces occupied the bridges of the Upper Thames at Radcot and Newbridge,

Gloucester, Warwick and Nottingham seized the Cotswold towns behind the line of de Vere's advance, causing the King's friend to fall into Derby's trap.

After a long march from Stow-on-the-Wold, de Vere was dismayed to find Henry Bolingbroke already in possession of Radcot Bridge. It was December 20th, a day of thick fog. This was fortunate for Derby and his men, for de Vere's army could not perceive them at first. Too late, Robert ordered the unfurling of the royal standard, but his men, sensing their imminent defeat, deserted in droves and fled the field. De Vere, no coward, realizing the position was hopeless, galloped furiously for his life along the banks of the Thames through Newbridge Forest. Finding it held by Bolingbroke's archers, he searched desperately for a ford. Near Bablock-Hythe, he freed himself from his heavy armour and, dragging his horse into the water - an icy experience on this December night - managed to escape to France. The brave Constable of Chester, Sir Thomas Molyneux, was either murdered after surrendering or during a parley by the appellants.

One eye witness of these historic events, on whom they made a great impression, was Adam of Usk, then engaged on his legal work in Oxford. How vivid was the scene as the Chronicler, by no means unsympathetic to the rebels' cause, watched the triumphant troops of the five lords appellant

> march through the city on their way to London from the battlefield, whereof the earls of Warwick and Derby led the van, the Duke of Gloucester the main body, and the earls of Arundel and Nottingham the rear.[22]

For Richard, the defeat and flight of Robert de Vere was a cruel and humiliating experience. The lonely young King, aged almost twenty-one, was in the Tower quite desolate, deprived of his dearest friends and at the mercy of the ruthless lords. He had reached the lowest ebb of his fortunes. Sir Simon Burley, old and infirm, was in prison; the Earl of Suffolk, disguised as a poultry seller, had escaped first to Holland and then to Paris, while the Archbishop of York had also been forced to flee to Louvain. John of Gaunt was still in Spain. Only Richard's Queen remained, a source of infinite comfort in his desperate state.

Having wisely secured the good will of the City of London, the lords appellant blockaded the Tower with its forces ranged round its walls, and the Londoners friendly with the soldiers. The December air was thick with menace and the clamour of the people.

The Earl of Northumberland and Archbishop Courtenay, now acting as intermediaries, arranged a parley for the five lords with King Richard in the Tower, carefully insuring that five hundred of their retainers remained on guard at the gates.

It was indeed fortunate for Richard that serious discord now arose between Gloucester and his ally, Arundel, and Mowbray (Nottingham) and Bolingbroke. While the King's younger uncle and Arundel were quite uncompromising, prepared for extreme measures, Derby and Nottingham were not dissatisfied, now that Richard had been humbled and his favourite ministers dismissed.

Outwardly, the lords showed every possible deference to the King, remaining on their knees until Richard, enthroned on a chair draped with cloth of gold, gave them the signal to rise, but their proud, arrogant demeanour, heavy armour and menacing swords belied their respectful behaviour. Exactly what passed between them is fascinating to conjecture, but we do not know for certain. The rebel lords bitterly reproached Richard for breaking his oath and allowing his friends to escape, accusing the King of contriving to kill them (the appellants), his true counsellors. They upbraided him for his adherence to "false traitors", to the undoing of his own safety and the weakening of the whole realm.[23] It is extremely unlikely that Richard, with his mystical and strongly held belief in his own 'régalitée', would have merely submitted to their demands. He would have argued, even protested. This may have been the second occasion when Gloucester not only threatened his nephew with deposition, but actually proclaimed him deposed "for two days or thre", an act of treason. If, as seems probable, Gloucester acted in such a way, it would have been resisted by Derby and Nottingham. Did Thomas of Woodstock plan to usurp his nephew's throne? It is clear that while his father remained in the Iberian, Richard's cousin Henry would never have allowed it. He was almost certainly in communication with his father at this time.

During the interview, Henry, Earl of Derby, took his cousin to a window and the sight of the hostile, ugly multitude outside induced him to yield. Richard held one valuable card. He could play off the divisions among the Lords Appellant, one against another. That evening, Richard asked Derby and Nottingham to supper with him, taking the opportunity to obtain their support for his old tutor Sir Simon Burley when he was brought to trial.

All the same, Richard was compelled to agree to very hard conditions, and for writs for a new Parliament to be summoned to meet at Westminster on February 3rd. It was to be known as the Merciless Parliament of 1388, one of the most brutal and infamous in our history. Richard, who had once defiantly informed his enemies that he would not dismiss the meanest of his scullions at their behest, was forced to dismiss not only his favourite Chamber Knights, Sir James Berners, John Salisbury, and Sir John Beauchamp, the Steward, Nicholas Dignall, and Sir Thomas Trivet, but even his personal clerks, his chaplain and his confessor. It did not matter that their only crime was loyalty to their King. And Burley was soon to face trial.

The Monk of Westminster relates a story about one of Richard's Knights, Sir James Berners, an intimate friend. On one occasion when the Court was at Ely during 1383, Richard had been present when Berners had been struck by lightning during a heavy thunderstorm. It left him "blind and half crazed". The King had then given orders that the clergy should go in reverent procession to the tomb of St. Ethelreda the Virgin in the lovely Norman cathedral. Only by means of sincere prayers of intercession could the blinded man recover his sight. Berners, himself, believed that he was certain to be condemned by the judges unless St. Ethelreda and St. John the Evangelist were to intervene on his behalf. It is ironic to know that Sir James regained his sight, only to become a victim of the vindictive Lords Appellant five years later.

For Richard, to be powerless while the five lords strode through the royal apartments in Westminster Palace, examining his accounts and hounding his closest friends to prison, was his ultimate humiliation. Others were banished from Court, such as Aubrey de Vere, Robert's uncle, Sir John Clanvowe, a poet, Sir John Golafre, an ambassador to the French Court during Richard's reign, and the Lords Camoys and de la Zouche. Supporters of the King such as John Fordham, Bishop of Durham, were similarly dealt with.

V   The Merciless Parliament

Both John Favent's *Historia Mirabilis* and *The Knighton Chronicle* are hostile to the King's friends and favourites. Favent gives a vivid picture of the scene at the Opening of Parliament: "The White Hall was very crowded. The Lords Appellant in their golden robes with their arms virtually interwined slowly advanced into the Chamber, bowing to the King as he sat on his throne." On his right sat the Lords Spiritual, on his left, the Lords Temporal. The hall was crammed with knights and burgesses. As Chancellor, the subtle Prelate, Thomas Arundel, took a leading part in the opening proceedings. None of the accused men were present at their trial. De Vere, Suffolk and Neville had escaped overseas, while Burley and Brembre were being held in prison, and Chief Justice Tressilian was in hiding.

Sir Robert Pleasington, formerly Chief Baron of the Exchequer, when presenting the case on behalf of the five appellants, declared them all free from the intent of treason. Though the Chancellor spoke on Richard's behalf, he was really the mouthpiece of the appellants. After Pleasington had said that there was no substance in the charge of the royal favourites that the Duke of Gloucester was guilty of treason, Arundel added with a slight touch of irony in his voice, that he came from such an honourable line and one so closely allied to the throne that no such suspicion could be held against him.

It fell to an official named Geoffrey Martyn to present the appellants' case. He might be described as one of the first non-political civil servants reading a document of thirty-nine articles written in French. To accuse Alexander Neville, Archbishop of York, Michael de la Pole, Earl of Suffolk, Robert de Vere, Duke of Ireland, Robert Tressilian, the Chief Justice, and Sir Nicholas Brembre, the City magnate of "high treasons made by them against the King and his Kingdom" was the height of absurdity. The clerk's voice droned on. They had taken advantage of the King's tender years and usurped the royal power, accusations that might have been just as applicable to Gloucester and his friends. The King no doubt had been over-generous to the accused noblemen and others of his friends, but there was no real proof they were guilty of corruption.

It is evident that in their eagerness to convict the King's friends, the Lords Appellant committed a grave miscarriage of justice. When asked by Parliament to give their opinion as to the legality of "the appeal for Treason", the judges and sergeants learned in the law courageously replied that it was illegal by every criterion known to them.[1] That did not deter Gloucester and his allies from declaring that the Lords, with the King's assent (he was then a mere puppet King), were the correct judges in such a case. It was highly convenient for the King's uncle to claim that in such high crimes which "touched the person of the King and the welfare of the Kingdom", judgement must be given by the Lords and Parliament, but there was no legal precedent in the late fourteenth century for this. To the rebel lords, the laws of Parliament as interpreted by themselves was superior to the Civil Law and the Common Law.

Miss M.V. Clark, in her scholarly *Fourteenth Century Studies*, is highly critical of the 1388 trials. In the fourteenth century, no extradition treaties existed between countries. In their absence, the accused were simply condemned to death without the semblance of fair trials. Sir Nicholas Brembre had undoubtedly abused the office of Mayor, interfering with the course of justice and creating riots among his opponents, so that he could be elected. Knighton is especially hostile, accusing Brembre of seizing eight thousand, five hundred Londoners and planning to behead them all. Presumably on behalf of King Richard, he had tried to raise an army in the City to oppose the Lords Appellant. He had intended to change the name of London to 'Little Troy', aspiring to be Duke of that city.

In the fourteenth century, the law was heavily weighted against the defendant. He was not only denied the right to see his indictment, but also the time to prepare his defence. Whatever were the ex-Lord Mayor's crimes, he certainly did not lack courage, for he made a spirited defence. He was no traitor. Richard did not desert Brembre in his dire need, making a valiant effort to save his friend. When various committees of peers found him innocent of the capital charge of treason, a more compliant court consisting of the new Mayor, the Aldermen and the Recorder of London reached a verdict that Brembre was more likely to be guilty of treason than not. This was hardly a satisfactory verdict, but enough for the ex-Lord Mayor to be condemned (February 1388).

Defiant to the end, Brembre claimed 'ordeal by battle', his privilege as a Knight to have the right to prove his innocence by mortal combat, but it was denied him, being only applicable where there were only witnesses against him. However, he had too many enemies in the City, resentful, among other things, that as a member of the Fishmongers' Guild he had kept the price of fish too high. Brembre was condemned to be hanged, but Richard pleaded for him that the sentence be commuted to beheading. Just before his execution, he admitted to a bystander, a follower of John of Northampton, his rival, that he had wronged him.

Unlike Brembre, Sir Simon Burley had many friends at Court. He was a Knight of the Garter, having held many high offices. Now fifty-two, considered old in that age, the King's former tutor, broken in health and hardly able to stand, was supported at the bar in Parliament by his nephew Sir Baldwin Raddington. Many members of the Commons were envious of Burley, because of the riches, honours and lands he had acquired from his master. There is probably some justification in Knighton's accusation that Sir Simon had been too lavish in his expenditures. While he had held office, his income had risen to over three thousand marks a year. Yet despite his apparent affluence, it is clear that Burley was in acute financial difficulties on the eve of the attack on the King's friends by the appellants. It is known that in 1387 and 1388, the last year of his life, Burley had raised money from six London citizens on the security of his clothes. At Christmas and other times he was wont to give costly liveries to arms-bearing Knights and esquires at Court. Perhaps he had encouraged Richard in his own fastidious and luxurious taste for dress, for he himself owned a tabard of cloth-of-gold embroidered with roses and lined with green tartarine. His coat armour of yellow and red is to this day still in Broad Arrow Tower. He owned a scarlet tabard embroidered with the sun and with gold letters, a white leather coat embroidered with the Burley badge and decorated with fifty-four golden buttons, an ermine cape and a cloak of pure minever.[2] Lavish dress was portable capital in those days, so that it could be used as security for loans.

Now "this right noble and courageous knight", as Froissart described him, was on trial for his life, hounded by the vindictive fury of the Duke of Gloucester. The Monk of Westminster tells us that the Duke of York, usually so indolent and spineless, showed boldness and courage in the White Hall, pleading in full Parliament that Burley had been in all his dealings loyal to the King and the realm. To anybody who wished to deny or gainsay this, he would himself give the lie and prove his point in personal combat.[3] A furious row now broke out between Gloucester and York. Thomas of Woodstock argued, on the other hand, that Burley had been false to his allegiance, offering to prove this with his sword-arm. The brothers would have hurled themselves upon one another had it not been for King Richard. By his quick and subtle diplomacy, the King succeeded in calming the irate noblemen.

The Monk of Westminster praises him for "his characteristic mildness and good will". Despite his passionate temper and lack of control, Richard, as he grew to manhood, could be diplomatic enough. However, the Lords were bitterly divided as to Burley, some championing him while others opposed him. Among those who pleaded for Burley's life after his condemnation was the Earl of Derby, and Sir Baldwin Raddington likewise did his utmost to save his uncle. Richard, too, fought desperately to prevent Gloucester and his partisans from wreaking their vengeance on his wretched old tutor.

In his misery, Richard even allowed his Queen to fall on her knees before his hardhearted uncle Gloucester to beg for mercy. There she remained for some time. She retained great affection for the old man. It was deeply humiliating. Gloucester merely told her that it would be more fitting if she were to pray for herself and her husband. He had insolently warned his nephew that while he clung to Burley he risked his throne. Burley was duly executed on May 5th, and Berners and Beauchamp, both Chamber Knights and devoted to the King, met the same fate. Burley's alleged treason was plotting the deaths of the Commission Council two years earlier.

68

Nobody was more hated than Sir Robert Tressilian, the Chief Justice: by the people because of the harsh sentences he had pronounced after the Peasants' Revolt and by the barons because of his interpretation of the law of treason in 1387, which directly threatened their lives. For a while, he had hidden himself in the house of an apothecary near the Westminster Gate. So skilful was his disguise, for he wore a shabby coat and grew a wide and long beard (known as a 'Parisian'), that nobody could recognize him, except for his voice. He might have passed for a poor, feeble old fellow. There are conflicting accounts in the Chronicles. Favent wrote that Tressilian was betrayed by the master of the house, when hidden under a round table covered with tattered cloths. Froissart's revelations are inaccurate, though the Chief Justice's alleged dialogue with the Duke of Gloucester bears witness to his skill as a story teller.

The Monk of Westminster wrote that Tressilian found sanctuary in the Church of St. Peter (Westminster Abbey), only to be arrested by Gloucester and others holding a deep grudge against the wretched fugitive. Sir Robert was not given a proper trial, having already been condemned by Parliament in his absence. He protested against his sentence. Dragged along the cobbled roads to Tyburn, he was stripped of his clothes by the executioner, his throat cut and hanged on Tyburn gallows, much to the delight of the bloodthirsty rabble. On his body were depicted the head of the devil, the names of devils and various signs of the Zodiac.

So, once more, another of Richard's friends had been liquidated. What angered and exasperated the King was the violation of the rights of sanctuary,[4] for he held very strong convictions concerning Westminster privileges. Whilst at his Palace of Kennington, the King ordered evidences of these privileges to be brought to him and read aloud in the hearing of the Chancellor Thomas Arundel (since April 3rd, Archbishop of York), William of Wykeham, the old, eminent Bishop of Winchester, Sir John Devereux, the royal Steward and others. The privilege of sanctuary was very ancient. As already recorded, Abbot Littlington had protested when the right of sanctuary had been violated in the case of Hauley and Shakel, formerly soldiers in the service of the Black Prince. The right depended on putative charters of two Saxon kings, Edgar and Edward the Confessor. Clearly it extended to somebody seeking protection in the Abbey for an alleged crime, though Parliament had provided in 1378 that fraudulent debt and trespass were excluded from the scope of sanctuary. The Chancellor Arundel had not the same scruples as Richard, being opposed altogether to the principle, thinking it right for a fugitive from justice to be dragged out of sanctuary. A measure of force should be used, if necessary, to remove a person's goods. He argued that despite the violation of sanctuary, these were properly forfeited to the royal Exchequer.

Richard, however, maintained that all those concerned in forcing Robert Tressilian to leave the Abbey, both those who had taken an active part and those who had acquiesced, should be excommunicated.

John Paule, a household servant and odd-job man employed in the Abbey, after being indicted for homicide four years later in 1392, confessed that he deserved to suffer death for his treachery in betraying the Chief Justice's secret hiding place in the sanctuary.[5]

A trial by battle occurred during May 1391 in ancient Tothill Street, Westminster, between two felons. One man accused the other of encouraging a fugitive seeking sanctuary in the Abbey to come out, whereupon he was treacherously arrested and ultimately hanged. Unfortunately, right did not prevail, for the accused man attacked his opponent so ferociously that he was thwarted in his attempt to gain a victory for what he honestly believed was the truth.

The Monk of Westminster praises Richard lavishly for championing the Church's liberties. "How this noble King reveres and loves God's Church!" he wrote. " . . . Why there is not a bishop so jealous as he is for the rights of the Church, so that on many occasions, but for him and him alone, she might have lost her privileges."[6]

Among minor officials sacrificed to the blood lust of the Lords Appellant was Thomas Usk, remembered today for his original poem *Testament of Love* written in 1386 or 1387 and wrongly attributed to Chaucer. It is described by Gervase Mathew as "a complete novelty in literary form, in prose, which was unprecedented for an allegory of love".[7] Thomas Usk's attitude to women was courtly, his poem being inspired by his love for a woman called Margarete. He owed his ruin to his support of Richard and the Court party. A former Secretary to John of Northampton from 1381 to 1383, in the following year he was imprisoned for sedition. However, he was released after being granted an interview with the King when he accused Northampton of treason. Usk apparently acted as a kind of intermediary with Richard's Court party and the followers of Nicholas Brembre, who favoured the royal policy. Owing to the King's influence, Usk became Under Sheriff of London. Retribution soon overtook him. When the Lords Appellant acquired control of the City they accused Usk of compiling false indictments for treason against the various lords and knights, members of the so-called Wonderful Parliament. He suffered at Tyburn, being hanged for his alleged offences.

The 'Merciless Parliament' was to last from early February till 1388. The tragedy for Richard was the cruel and brutal execution of his dearest friends, leaving him strangely isolated. Yet in the harsh school of adversity, Richard was to learn many lessons, among them to dissemble, and the necessity to bide his time for revenge.

The Monk of Westminster relates how at a solemn service consisting of a Mass and sermon held in Westminster Abbey on June 3rd, the King was made to renew his coronation oath, first sworn at his Coronation eleven years ago. Why was this necessary? It would seem to strengthen the hypothesis that Richard had earlier been deposed for three days to have warranted such a ceremony taking place. While the leading men of the kingdom stood by, Richard sat ensconced on his throne before the high altar while Robert Braybrook, Bishop of London, officiated at the Mass.

He was still a complete cypher, being forced to submit his personal affairs to a governing committee consisting of Braybrook, the Bishop of Winchester, the Earl of Warwick, Lord Cobham and Richard Scrope of Bolton in Yorkshire. The Lords Appellant, loath to relinquish their powers, continued to deal with affairs, although after one year their Commission's legal title had not been renewed.

Despite their constant exhortations to Richard to cease his extravagance, the appellants certainly lined their pockets. Parliament voted them £20,000 "for their great expenses".[8]

During April, Richard's half-brother, Sir John Holland, returned from Spain after giving distinguished service to John of Gaunt. He seems, outwardly at least, to have supported the appellants at this juncture, for he was richly rewarded with the Earldom of Huntingdon and given an allowance of 2,000 marks per annum.[9] Despite their bitterness and persecution of the King's advisers, the appellants achieved very little while they remained in power. They were no statesmen. Their only real success was the naval expedition against France in June 1388, when the Earl of Arundel, appointed Admiral of England, captured eighty enemy ships and masses of booty.

VI   Richard's Personal Rule

Taking advantage of the strife in England and knowing that the country was ill-prepared to resist invasion, the Scots during August 1388 mounted raids against Northumberland and Cumberland. The Commander of the Scots army was James, Second Earl of Douglas, aged thirty-eight at this period, a valiant, experienced and resourceful soldier, with a reputation for prudence. His forces consisting of 3,000 cavalry and 2,000 infantry rapidly advanced on Newcastle, the most populous town in Northumbria. When tidings reached the Earl of Northumberland at Alnwick Castle, his responsibility was to protect the border country from invasion - he summoned his two sons, the charismatic Hotspur (Sir Harry Percy) and Sir Ralf, his younger son, to Alnwick. "Ye shall go to Newcastle (a distance of twenty-nine miles) and all the county shall assemble there," he told them, "and I shall tarry at Alnwick."[1] It is still a lovely place with its rugged old Castle, superbly situated overlooking the river Aln.

Otterburn in Redesdale is the scene of the famous, bloody battle fought on a sweet moonlit night, August 15th, during Lammas-tide, six hundred years ago. It owes its lustre and its magic to the poets and ballad writers inspired by the bravery of Sir Harry Percy fighting against his hereditary noble enemy James Earl of Douglas, chivalrous even in death, for he was killed in the battle. Otterburn, or Chevy Chase as it is sometimes called, has been immortalized by Jean Froissart and in the late eighteenth century by Bishop Thomas Percy in his *Reliques of English Poetry*. He always proudly claimed that he was a descendant of Sir Thomas Percy (later Earl of Worcester). Sir Philip Sidney, writing in the *Defence of Poesie* in the late sixteenth century says: "I never heard the old song of Percy and Douglas, that I founde not my heart mooved more than with a Trumpet."[2] He was listening to some poor blind musician (crowder) playing a plaintive air on the harp.

I can never read the noble passage in Froissart where Sir Ralf Percy is taken prisoner without emotion. His captor was a Scots Knight, Sir John Maxwell. He was desperately wounded. "Pray take some heed to me for I am sore hurt, gasped Sir Ralf, my drawers and my greaves are full of blood."[3] Despite the brutality there was chivalry in medieval warfare. Percy was taken care of by Maxwell's men. Hotspur, fighting in another part of the battlefield was also captured having been wounded, after a stubborn fight with his captor, Sir John Montgomery. High ransoms were customary in those days for illustrious prisoners, so Montgomery was able to demand £3,000. It is said that he bought with the ransom money a castle in Renfrewshire.

Hotspur was no great strategist, too impulsive in the opening gambits. The Scots were the victors at Otterburn, though the Northumbrians were loath to admit defeat. There exists today only the Percy Cross to commemorate the battle, but the place is pervaded by a vast stillness and sadness where dramatic scenes have occurred. Sir Harry was richly rewarded for his services by his grateful King. He was created not only a Knight of the Garter, but Governor of Carlisle and Warden of the West Marches. His father Northumberland and uncle Sir Thomas Percy had already been given the Garter, so the three Percies are the only members of a family to receive the honour at the same time.

He was soon released. According to de Fonblanque, an authority on the Percies in Northumberland, so greatly did the English Parliament value his services that they were prepared to advance £1,000 towards his ransom. Most people think of him only as a great warrior, skilled in arms, but Richard used him on one occasion on a complimentary mission to Cyprus in 1393. A letter from King James of Cyprus to Richard reveals how much he appreciated the services of such a graceful and noble envoy as "dominus Henricus Percy". Otterburn had no lasting results. Though there might have been a temporary lull, the bitter internecine warfare would continue for very many years.

The pages of Holinshed are full of strange occurrences. During the hot days of July 1388, Richard was at one of his favourite palaces, Sheen, where

> there swarmed together in his Court great multitude of flies and gnats, insomuch that in manner of skirmishing they en-

74

countered each other; and making great slaughters on both sides were in the end swept awaie from the place where they laie dead.

By the early autumn, disillusion in Parliament concerning the appellants was widespread. In opposition, incessantly mouthing their grievances against the Court party, they had enjoyed considerable popularity, but fierce criticism of their lack of statesmanship was now mounting.

The Monk of Westminster has a full account of the only Parliament to be held at Cambridge, assembling on September 19th at Barnwell Priory and lasting till October 17th. It dealt with three important medieval social problems: the practice of livery and maintenance, the wages and mobility of labour and the responsibility for the poor, and the sanitation of towns.[4] One of the great evils of the time was the private armies of baronial retainers, a constant threat to law and justice. The Commons, however, attacked both royal and baronial livery, the emblem of the White Hart worn by the adherents to Richard II and the various badges such as the swan, the horse, and the bear issued by the lords

since those who wear them are by reason of the power of their masters flown with such insolent arrogance that they do not shrink from practising with reckless effrontery various forms of extortion in the surrounding countryside, fleecing and discomforting the poor in every court.[5]

Richard's suggestion to the Cambridge Parliament that he would be prepared to do without his own white hart showed his intelligence. He calculated rightly that Gloucester and his friends would object to a law depriving them of the sources of their power. Never would they agree to it. In their stubborn refusal they antagonized the Commons, resulting in the King drawing closer to the Lower House. Parliament now enacted that all cognizances more recent in origin than the accession of Edward III should cease, but the law proved difficult to administer. The feudal, private armies remained for many years until the Tudors were strong enough to do away with them.

Richard can hardly be blamed for the harsh legislation enacted in the Statute of Labourers (1388) and imposed on the working man and vagrants. The Lords Appellant were still in power. The Monk of Westminster relates:

> No labourer or serving-man or woman of whatsoever estate or condition he be, shall at the end of his term depart out of the town where he dwells to serve or dwell in another town without sealed letters from the Justices of the Peace under pain of forty days imprisonment. The wretched beggars were treated as runaway labourers. No labourer or servant of any craftsman or victualler was allowed to carry baselard, dagger or sword upon pain of forfeiture of these weapons. All those who contravened these laws would be arrested by the sheriffs, mayors, bailiffs and constables and brought before Justices of the Peace. No labourer was allowed to be taught a craft, if required to serve at the plough or on the land.[6]

The statutory wages were very low, the carter earning 10s per annum, the shepherd 10s, the oxherd 6s 8d, the cowherd 6s 8d, the woman labourer 6s and the dairymaid 6s.

Evidently the knights and burgesses in 1388 had no more sympathy for the poor than the barons and bishops. Indeed there is no reason to think that Richard's attitude towards the poor differed from that of his contemporaries. All the same, his Statute of Mortmain enacted during his early personal rule (1391) was enlightened legislation; it provided that a proportion of the fruits of benefice appropriated to a monastery should be distributed to the poor of the parish.[7] However, the mass of people were not represented in Parliament. The policy adopted towards the underprivileged can best be understood when one takes into account that the ruling class had not recovered from the rude shock of the Peasants' Revolt.

One beneficial statute passed, the Statute of Barnwell, dealt with a pressing problem - the total lack of sanitation in medieval towns and villages. It is important because it became the first urban sanitary Act in our history. Attempts were at least made to remove the filthy dung and refuse from the streets. It is difficult for us in the late twentieth century to imagine the nauseating odours pervading the highways. The Chancellor of Cambridge University, for instance, was required by writ "to remove from the streets and lanes of the town all swine, and all dirt, dung, filth and trunks and branches of trees, and to cause the streets and lanes to be kept clean for the future".[8]

By January 1389, it was imperative to strengthen the border defences. For this purpose Richard appointed Thomas Mowbray, Earl of Nottingham, the Earl Marshal, Warden of the East March. Now restored to favour, though the King never really forgave him for siding with the rebel lords, Northumberland, the most powerful magnate in the north, possessing the immense prestige of the Percies, was created Warden of the West March.

Richard was, by now, as eager for the return of his elder uncle, the Duke of Lancaster, as he had once been glad to get rid of him. Gaunt had abandoned his own ambitions, having achieved two brilliant marriages for his daughters, Philippa, now Queen of Portugal, and Katharine, married to Henry of Castile. He was immensely wealthy, including the 600,000 gold francs he now received from abroad. However, Gloucester and his friends intrigued to keep him out of England as long as possible.

On May 3rd 1389, Richard acted with a touch of instinctive brilliance and political realism, revealing a characteristic love of the dramatic. At a meeting of the Great Council at Westminster, he confronted the astonished lords, demanding of them how old he was. His uncle Gloucester, as their spokesman, answered that he had turned twenty. The King replied in this fashion, quick to outwit the malignant Gloucester and his allies:

> Therefore I am of full age to govern myself, my household and my realm, for it seems wrong to me that I should be treated with less consideration than the meanest of my subjects. For what heir in my realm when he has passed his twentieth year and his parent is dead, is prevented from freely conducting his own affairs? Why therefore deny me what is conceded to others of lesser rank?[9]

Its logic was indeed difficult to refute. The Lords in Council were compelled to acquiesce.

It was a moment of triumph. Frustrated at every turn by his opponents, ambitious barons, the King had at last come into his own. Reared in a harsh school, Richard was learning a political finesse, a subtlety and cunning in dealing with them, hitherto unsuspected. During the long years of humiliation he had learnt much from his failures and mistakes. He had a long memory. While he would often feign friendship with those who had wronged him, he was really planning the best means to revenge their insults. Like his father, the Black Prince, he never forgave.

One commentator thinks that Richard's initiative in his sudden announcement that he would personally assume the government of his kingdom was one of those spurts of action which marked the pattern of his behaviour throughout his life. Undoubtedly he was both impulsive and at times unstable, but he was at the same time calculating, prepared to bide his time, ready to strike when the hour was ripe.

Richard's calculated revenge, however, has on the whole been little understood by historians. As the writer - a monk of the *Kirkstall Chronicle* wrote (he came from Yorkshire), Richard "with marvellous and long-lasting patience (*admirabilis et diutiurna paciencia*) now made a vow to avenge the executions and exiles of his closest friends". Perhaps the impulsive, the unpredictable, element in his character has been stressed too much. It is a fatal misunderstanding to regard his later actions as the frenzy of a mad man. Only from 1397 did he show signs of neurotic behaviour, exasperated as he was by the disloyalty of Gloucester, Arundel and others.

He was no bad judge when assuming power and making his first appointments. William of Wykeham, founder of Winchester College and New College, Oxford, replaced the Archbishop of York as Chancellor, while Gloucester and Warwick were left out of the Council. The King's half-brother, now the Earl of Huntingdon, having been restored to Richard's favour, replaced Arundel as Admiral and Captain of Brest, while Richard showed his interest in Ireland by appointing Sir John Stanley, formerly the Duke of Ireland's deputy, as Justice. It would have been foolish in the prevailing circumstances for Richard to recall his friends Robert de Vere, Suffolk and Archbishop Neville from exile. Robert was well entertained at the French Court by Charles VI until his father-in-law de Coucy, who hated him for his treatment of his daughter Philippa, persuaded Charles together with other French noblemen to expel him. Both de Vere and Neville lived in Louvain. Suffolk died in exile in Paris in 1389.

The sour-faced Walsingham, insular and narrow-minded, cannot resist his venom, calling Suffolk "that server of treachery, that sink of avarice, that charioteer of treason", even accusing him of being a traitor to his fatherland. It is hard to distinguish the truth in such a welter of falsehood.

Richard made one excellent appointment. Edmund de Stafford, aged about forty-one, a distinguished scholar and patron of learning, was created Keeper of the Privy Seal.[10] A founder of Exeter College, Oxford, Richard later appointed him Bishop of Exeter. De Stafford, an able administrator, wisely steered clear of being involved in any faction. The office of Keeper of the Privy Seal was the focal point of government. His appointments were not at first in the least revolutionary. Indeed he seemed almost to want to appease the appellants. Within a few months of Richard's assumption of full power, he had restored Gloucester, Arundel and Warwick to the Council. He made no attempt to cancel the £20,000 voted by Parliament to be paid the appellants.

The King was anxious for his uncle John of Gaunt to return to England, but it was not until Richard had sent him an urgent summons that Gaunt complied. His early unpopularity was now no more, for most people regarded him as a venerable personality, a respected elder statesman. When the Duke of Lancaster landed at Plymouth on November 19th, he made preparations to attend the King's Council at Reading on December 10th. Richard met him outside the town, giving him the kiss of peace. It was a State occasion. Gaunt rode in a triumphal procession to Westminster where William Colchester, the Abbot, accompanied by the monks in black Benedictine gowns, preceded him to the high altar. Another service followed at St. Paul's.

He excelled in diplomacy rather than in warfare. Consequently, the King made use of his uncle to reconcile him with the appellants. Gaunt himself made peace with the Earl of Northumberland.

It is fascinating to conjecture what John of Gaunt really thought of the decisive part his son Henry had taken against King

Richard during the Merciless Parliament. The position is baffling and very confused. Derby would have consulted his father, informed him of his moves. Did his father, perhaps, express disapproval or even anger? It is certain that he discussed him with Richard. The invaluable French source *Chronique de la Traison et Mort de Richard II*, definitely anti-Lancastrian and occasionally betraying bias, maintains that the Duke of Lancaster on several occasions pressed the King to execute his cousin for his part in the rebellion.[11] It is likely that to humour Richard, his uncle may have made some such remark as "he deserves to die", but he almost certainly never intended the King to take him literally. Bolingbroke's most recent biographer says that Gaunt's devotion to his eldest son never wavered.[12]

John Hardyng, Harry Hotspur's faithful squire, a partisan of the Percies, too young to serve his master at Otterburn but present later at the battles of Homildon Hill and Shrewsbury, alleges in his Chronicle that John of Gaunt put forward a claim in Parliament to be recognized heir apparent to King Richard, "considering how the King was like to have no issue of his body". The Commons, however, maintained that Roger Mortimer, Earl of March, descended from Edward III's third son, Lionel of Clarence, was Richard's heir to the Crown. They would not agree to it. Then Hardyng accused Gaunt of forging a chronicle in which he alleged that his ancestor Edmund Crouchback, Henry III's younger son, was in reality the elder brother of Edward I. An absurd story which lacked further corroboration. There seems to be more substance in Hardyng's later accusation that Henry Bolingbroke in 1399 tried to make use of this Chronicle to prove his hereditary right to the Crown - incidentally, without success. That Gaunt should make such an ambitious claim seems extremely unlikely, for it would have surely aroused Richard's former fears and resentment against his uncle.[13] No doubt Hotspur often confided in his squire, John Hardyng, but he can hardly be described as unbiased, and would have been capable of embellishing what he had heard.

Even Richard's critics concede that for the first eight years "he wielded the power which thus passed quietly into his hands with singular wisdom and good fortune".[14]

Many historians have, however, discussed Richard as if he was an eighteenth century Hanoverian king instead of a medieval monarch. He certainly never regarded himself as a constitutional king, nor did he believe in democracy. There is substance, however, in Bishop Stubb's rhetorical question: "Was Richard shamming a belief in constitutional government in order to lull his enemies into a carelessness that would bring them to their death?" Yet the King was humane, for there were few executions during his reign.

Nobody can possibly understand Richard unless they see him as a king dedicated to reform. His ultimate object was to establish a regime of royal absolutism. As he conceived it, this would restore monarchy in England to its rightful place.[15] In two respects, at least, Richard had the makings of a statesman: in his enlightened pursuit of a lasting peace with France despite the bitter opposition of the more reactionary barons, and in his Irish policy. He had the insight to realize how wasteful and costly the war with France was. His own inclinations were strongly for peace.

No nobleman in the kingdom was more suited to represent his country in the negotiations than John of Gaunt. He was to give Richard loyal service for the rest of his life. He had the grand manner and a consummate experience of diplomacy, knowing personally all the most important personalities in France, the Dukes of Berry, Burgundy, Brittany and the King of Navarre. As the father of the Queen of Portugal and the Queen of Castile, he had enormous prestige. Accompanying Lancaster to France in March 1392 were his son the Earl of Derby, his brother York, Huntingdon and Sir Thomas Percy, so versatile and skilled in diplomacy. The negotiations proved long and arduous.

Charles VI, who was to receive Lancaster so hospitably at Amiens, was then aged twenty-four, about the same age as Richard. Both had succeeded to their thrones in boyhood. He was above average height, but not so tall as the King of England. Both monarchs delighted in the rituals of chivalry, but Charles took more pleasure in shining and polished arms than in jewels. He resembled Richard in his generosity to his friends. Whether or not "he was the victim of carnal appetites" (as alleged by the Monk of St. Denis), Froissart wrote that when he married his German bride Isabeau of Bavaria in July 1385 he was so eager to get into bed with her, "and if they passed that night together in great delight, one can well believe it".[16] An American author wrote: "No such eager marriage was ever to sink to a sudden end, in madness, debauchery and hate."[17]

It is related how poor Charles was smitten with intermittent madness. He developed an invincible aversion for his wife and Isabeau, naturally wanton, sought consolation in adultery and political intrigue. Such was Richard's future father-in-law.

Richard supported his uncle in every possible way to achieve peace with France. The protracted negotiations eventually led to the Truce of Lelinghen (May 24th 1394). The Duke of Gloucester's faction bitterly opposed Richard's French policy.

The King often longed for his exiled friend Robert de Vere, but it would have been madness to recall him. It was a real tragedy to hear that he had been killed in an accident during a boar hunt near Louvain in 1392. Richard's loyalty to de Vere reveals an attractive aspect of his complex character. He had his body brought back from Louvain and reinterred in the family vault at Earls Colne in Essex. As he looked on the embalmed face of his friend, Richard experienced renewed grief. His passionate temperament has been little understood. Determined to honour the dead man and showing how bitterly he resented the stigma of traitor passed on his favourite by the Merciless Parliament, Richard was present at a magnificent ceremony. Who can tell what thoughts surged in his mind as, with a theatrical gesture, he set a ring on de Vere's finger? Was it then that he made a renewed solemn vow that he would avenge the wrongs done to his friend? It was hardly surprising that several of his enemies - Gloucester, Warwick, Derby and Arundel - ostentatiously refused to attend.

Coleridge stresses Richard's "intensity of woman-like love of those immediately about him" and the need to lean for support on others, but he was no homosexual. *The Cambridge Medieval History* "dubs him, moody, violent, with melodramatic tastes, a high notion of his prerogative".[18]

From 1389 onwards a new favourite, Richard's first cousin Edward, eldest son of the Duke of York, was to take de Vere's place in Richard's affections. In that year, Edward - Richard created him Earl of Rutland in 1390 - was aged sixteen. Perhaps in some strange way his physical appearance or some trait of character may have reminded Richard of his beloved friend. He had been married in childhood in the cathedral of Portugal to Beatrix of Portugal, but the marriage had been annulled. As was his wont, Richard loaded Rutland with honours. He created him Admiral Warden of the Cinque Ports, Lord of the Isle of Wight and Warden of the Forests south of the Trent. Since he realized that his cousin possessed skill in diplomacy, Richard used him in negotiations with the Elector Palatine and the Archbishop of Cologne, finding Edward's links with the Court in Paris, invaluable. Rutland realized that his power and influence depended entirely on the King's favour and friendship. Whether he ultimately betrayed his master in Ireland is uncertain, but his act of abandoning Richard in extreme adversity was that of a man of duplicity, showing no gratitude for the favours heaped on him. Those familiar with Shakespeare's *Richard II* will see Rutland portrayed in the character of the Duke of Aumerle.

Richard II has been compared to Henry III as a lover of beautiful things,[1] but he must not be regarded as a dilettante. He was a connoisseur of architecture, sculpture, books, music and painting, a man who delighted in lavish dress, exquisite jewelry, embroidery, plate and exotic cooking. Whatever views we may have of his controversial character as a king, there is no doubt whatsoever that Richard's influence on the medieval art of the late fourteenth century was extremely beneficial.

It was no accident that Richard's reign may be considered the most splendid in the history of English medieval art on panel, for he was an eminent patron of artists and writers, actively encouraging them in their work. Dr. Joan Evans wrote: "A highly civilized Court may not be the best thing for a country's political welfare, but it helps to polish and refine a native art as nothing else can." Usurpers are usually too occupied in keeping their kingdoms to have much time for the arts.[2] Henry IV did not possess the impeccable artistic taste of his cousin and a visible deterioration ensued in 1400.

The Forme of Cury, the first cookery book, was compiled about 1390 by Richard's master cook.[3] As a renowned 'gourmet' he has been described as "the best and ryallest vyander of alle cristen kynges". A 'vyander' is a provider of viands, while the verb *curare* means in Latin not only to cure a distemper, but also to dress victuals. This little volume has a curious history. It came into the possession of the family of Lord Stafford, being presented to Queen Elizabeth I in the twenty-eighth year of her reign. Richard's first and second cooks held positions of importance at Court, being entitled to call themselves esquires. Richard was fastidious, so it is likely that he was a delicate eater, though the editor of *The Forme of Cury* rather tartly implies otherwise. It was customary for the courtiers to use spoons or their fingers.

The book consists of 196 recipes. The cuisine at Court was influenced by that of France. Entire joints of meat were never served, fish and fowl being usually hacked and cut into pieces or gobbets. A characteristic pottage was venison broth. 'The maw-menee', the main course, might consist of minced flesh of pheasant, richly spiced with cinnamon, cloves and ginger and Greek wine would be added. A typical favoured dish was shelled oysters and hares' flesh, flavoured with honey.[4] Deer's livers and hares' flesh often formed the basis of enormous pâtés, while another recipe was of gele (jelly) of fish consisting of eel and turbot. Olive oil rather than butter formed the basis of cooking and 'lumbard mustard' from Italy was very popular. Saffron is often mentioned, imported from Egypt, Cilicia or other parts of the Levant and much used, and also for colouring and garnishing. Sir Walter Besant mentioned roast hares, herons and egrettes (a kind of heron) as forming part of a medieval feast.[5] Cranes thrived in damp and marshy places and were either trapped or shot with a bow for a single feast.

Here is a typical recipe: 'Take pork yfrude and gryde it small with safron medle (mix) it with agren and raisins of Coraunce and powda fort and salt and make a soile of dowh.' Sweets or savouries were known as 'sotiltees', and one much favoured was mulberries cooked with honey.

The courtiers were partial to Rhenish wines, and wine from La Rochelle. Another much appreciated was Vernage, a strong white wine from Northern Italy. Richard himself planted vines at Windsor, producing large quantities of wines, some of which were sold and the remainder drunk at Court.[6] The Vale of Gloucester produced the most choice wines. However, this industry gradually fell into disuse because it was discovered that wine could be imported from Bordeaux more cheaply and better than it could be produced at home.

In the towns, craftsmen, cooks and their valets chanted: "Hot pies, good pigs and geese, white wine of Alsace, red wine of Gascony."

It was customary after ceremonial dinners both at Richard's Court and the Court of Charles VI of France to offer hypocras, wine and comfits. These were offered in boxes of silver or gold, and consisted of nuts, paste du roy, citron, sugar-plums and all sorts of delectable things. At a dinner held in Westminster during 1397 when Richard was about to depart for Bristol, some soldiers who had held Brest for the King, arrived home. It is related that the King took comfits and wine after dinner.[7]

While the name of Richard's master cook is not known, we do know that of the King's tailor, Walter Raufe. After the King had pensioned his nurse Mundina Danos of Aquitaine in 1378, she had married Raufe. In his generous way, Richard contrived to give them small gifts.

Richard may justly be charged with extravagance for the foppish dress worn by himself and for the quickly changing fashions of his Court. It seems evident that Court dress became magnificent during Richard's personal rule from 1390 onwards. He owned, for instance, a dress worth more than £1,000, more than a hundred times the amount today. Fairly late in his reign - say in 1394 - a successful courtier would have worn a shirt and short drawers (braies) made of fine linen.[8] It came usually from Paris, Rheims and Dinant. The under doublet, the 'gipon', was worn to protect the courtier against the cold. The 'houpelandes' mentioned by contemporary writers were particularly magnificent, high-necked gowns "that fell to the knees and at times almost to the ankles". A manuscript[9] in the British Library depicts brightly coloured blue houpelandes, embroidered with different patterns in gold and silver. One described by Thomas Hoccleve is a scarlet houpelande edged with fur costing more than £20.

An inventory of the possessions of Simon Burley shows how magnificently the courtiers lived. Among Sir Simon's articles of clothing were eight fur cloaks or gowns, and a tabard of scarlet with a sleeve embroidered with the sun and letters of gold and lined with white tartarine.[10] All the great magnates owned splendid beds, Burley one of green tartarine, embroidered with ships and birds. It later came into the possession of Richard Medford, Bishop of Salisbury, and the King bought it from him for £13 6s 8d.[11]

The King's taste for lavish jewels was imitated by important courtiers such as Sir Thomas Percy, Vice-Chamberlain of the royal household and Royal Steward since 1394. An inventory exists showing that Sir Thomas possessed a gold circlet garnished with

Portrait of Richard II, earliest known contemporary wooden panel-painting of an English king, attributed to André Beauneveu, portrait painter to the King of France.

Boy King attempting to land at Rotherhithe during the Peasants' Revolt (1381).

Richard II handing the Charter granted to the City of Shrewsbury (1389) to his first Queen Anne of Bohemia, confirming privileges already granted by Edward III.

Jean Froissart presents his Chronicle to Richard II at Leeds Castle.

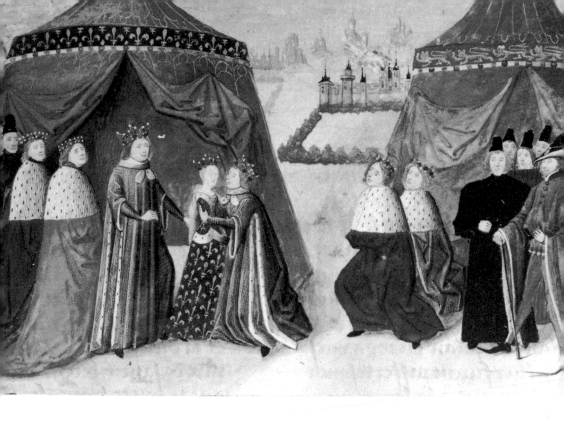

Richard II greets his child bride and second Queen, Isabelle of France.

Richard II rides out of London with his men-at-arms intending to quell the rebellion in Ireland.

The Earl of Northumberland arrests Richard II in North Wales.

Tomb and effigies of Richard II (1399) and Anne of Bohemia (1394).

emeralds, a jewel that consisted of one emerald, three rubies and three sapphires, pearls, sapphires and rubies with a diamond in its centre and a girdle set with gems.[12] Percy, like his master, was a patron of Jean Froissart. It is probable that Richard's personal emblem, the badge of the white hart which he did not adopt until 1390, was used because a white hind had once been the emblem of his mother, Princess Joan. Among the King's jewels were three brooches of the white hart. Richard's half-brother, the Earl of Huntingdon, later Duke of Exeter, owned 'a livery of the hart' set with three rubies and two sapphires worn in his dress.

The shoes worn by the courtiers were highly absurd, and subject to ridicule, for their pointed toes were of inconvenient length. They were called 'cracowes' since the fashion was probably derived from the ancient city of Cracow in Poland.

The fashion set by ladies of the Court was more conservative than the men's. There were a great number of ladies at Richard's Court, wearing gaudy silk gowns; they gracefully mounted their palfreys as they rode side-saddle, moving from palace to palace according to the whim of the King. Indeed, their excessive number was much criticized because of the cost to the kingdom. Men painted their cheeks at Court, as well as women.

Richard bore only a superficial resemblance to his forebear Edward II, though they shared various artistic interests. Throughout his life Edward was the keen patron of musicians and minstrels, being devoted to theatricals. Similarly, Richard often attended performances of plays, together with his Queen Anne, and himself "composed lays, ballads, songs and rondels".[13] On one occasion in 1380, he presented John Katerine, a Venetian dancing-master with ten marks. There the resemblance ceased. Richard held very lofty conceptions of his dignity, very distinct ideas of the powers, of the functions and of the duties of royalty, while Edward II had little dignity and no kingly aspirations whatever.[14] Where Richard once having attained personal power and the makings of a statesman, Edward would have been happiest in private life, working preferably with his hands as a rural craftsman, delighting in the company of thatchers, blacksmiths, carters and ditchers.[15] He had the saving grace of humour. Jack of St. Albans, the royal painter - a real Jester - gave him much enjoyment when he danced on the table, making Edward 'laugh beyond measure'. The King rewarded him with 50 shillings.

Edward was by no means a saint, but from 1387 onwards Richard had resolved to get his great grandfather canonized. For this purpose, the King had sent all sorts of envoys on missions to the Papal Court at Rome to plead Edward's claim to sanctity. His motive was a little obscure, but having earlier on been threatened, twice at least, with deposition, the King probably calculated that it would prove a powerful weapon against his enemies. If Edward were to be canonized, surely nobody would use that King's deposition in 1327 as an argument that it might act as a precedent for his own deposition.

According to the Monk of Westminster, the new Pope Boniface IX,[16] a Neapolitan, had earlier addressed a Bull to the Bishop of London, ordering him to inquire into the genuineness of the alleged miracles performed at Edward's magnificent tomb in Gloucester Cathedral. There, for some years, pilgrims had testified to the miraculous cures performed. During the autumn (1390), Richard rode to Gloucester where he was met by the Archbishop of Canterbury, the Bishop of London and various clergy and lawyers to collect stories of alleged miracles at the tomb to support his case. Fortunately, this superb tomb with its graceful canopy of Purbeck marble and local oolitic limestone survives. Richard failed to realize his ambition because the papal lawyers, never partial to rapid action, made delays. So the King's ardent efforts to brand his predecessor's death a crime were frustrated.

Richard had the choice of many palaces. One favourite home bequeathed to him by the Black Prince was Kennington[17] where he and his mother sometimes lived during the early days. It lay near Lambeth in South London. There, Richard had resided after the death of his father (June 1376) under the care of Princess Joan and the tutorship of Sir Guichard d'Angle. John of Gaunt had sought refuge there after his bitter quarrel with Bishop Courtenay of London. Many years later during October 1396, when Richard married his child-queen, the Princess Isabelle, eldest daughter of Charles VI, he had her brought to Kennington. Nearby at Blackheath, the royal party was met by the Mayor and aldermen, resplendently dressed, so as to honour Richard's little bride.

Of far more importance in the life of our Plantagenet King and his beloved first Queen, Anne, was the Palace of Sheen. The name is derived from a Saxon word meaning beautiful. Richard inherited Sheen from his grandfather Edward III, who had spent £2,000 on converting the royal manor of Kingston in Surrey into a palace and subsequently died at Sheen. Richard and Anne enjoyed their happiest hours in this enchanting place. There on an island named La Neyt, the King built a Royal Lodging between 1384 and 1388.[18] Sheen contained every shade of luxury and refinement, baths with large bronze taps for hot and cold water. The King commissioned 2,000 painted tiles for the chamber used for 'the King's bath'. H.M. Colvin tells us that other bronze taps providing hot and cold water were in use in Westminster Palace.[19] He made many improvements, commissioning elegant fireplaces in most of the rooms. The three great houses built by the King for his courtiers contained nine chambers, each possessing an elegant latrine. It is obvious that the courtiers were accustomed to a high standard of comfort. However, Richard was to experience a great personal tragedy at Sheen, utterly devastating in its impact on his character. With his hypersensitive, artistic temperament, we cannot wonder that he could no longer bear to live there after 1394, since it reminded him too poignantly of the idyllic days he had passed there with Anne.

Somehow, it is much easier to imagine Richard at Eltham Palace near Blackfriars, now for the most part a picturesque ruin.[20] All that survives of the medieval palace are the moat walls on the south and west sides, and the bases of two octagonal towers. In 1297, the manor was owned by Anthony Bec, Bishop of Durham, no friend of Edward I, but amiable to his son, our first Prince of Wales. Bec presented Eltham to Edward after he succeeded his father; and Edward III turned it into a palace. Richard II was very fond of Eltham and made frequent visits there, hunting in its park which then abounded with game, and entertaining on a grand scale. It is recorded that Leo VI, King of Armenia, visited Richard there in 1386 when he wanted the King's help in his war against the Turks. According to the Monk of Westminster, Richard was most generous, taking Leo to the monastery. Under the flickering candlelight, so austerely beautiful, the two Kings made their offerings.

Richard, dressed in "his more impressive finery", showed the admiring King the royal insignia with which he had been invested at his Coronation.[21]

Richard had the wooden bridge over the moat replaced by a stone one and it was there that Richard and his queen would pass fleeting, happy hours in the new turf garden made "for the pleasure of the King and his Queen Anne". Richard made many innovations at Eltham, adding a new bathhouse, a dancing chamber, exquisite stained glass and a so-called painted chamber.

For some years Geoffrey Chaucer was Clerk of Works for the Greenwich area and came to know Eltham well. And it was here that John of Gaunt, in chain armour, confronted his nephew, accusing the King's advisers of a plot to murder him. He had his own apartments at Eltham, as had Robert de Vere in his heyday and Thomas Mowbray. Lady Luttrell, fittingly described as "the mother of the maids of honour", also had her own apartments. King Henry IV later became attached to Eltham, adding a study to house his library. He was married to his second wife, Joanne of Navarre, in the Chapel, now no more.

Wishing to give pleasure to his Queen, Richard presented Anne with three royal manors, Leeds Castle near Maidstone in Kent, Woodstock in Oxfordshire, given to her in dower in 1382, and Havering in Essex, but it is not known whether she visited them. Edward II's Queen Isabella, the "she-wolf of France", much to her fury had once been refused admittance to Leeds Castle when on her way to Canterbury. Much loved by the early Plantagenet Queens, Leeds still remains ethereal and lovely. Jean Froissart, when returning to England in 1395, relates how he was presented to King Richard in his Chamber in Leeds Castle through the good offices of Sir Thomas Percy and the King's uncle, the Duke of York. It was here that Richard II signed the decrees against the Lollards. On this occasion Froissart took the opportunity of presenting Richard with a richly illustrated book. When asked its subject, the Chronicler delighted the King when he said "about love". The Hainaulter, so disparaging about Richard in the days of his downfall, stresses how affable and charming he was, and that he spoke to him in fluent French. He possessed a sensibility far in advance of his age. A first edition of Froissart's *Chronicles* is at Leeds Castle.

Richard sometimes went to another palace, King's Langley in Hertfordshire, once the favourite home of Edward II. His beloved "brother Perrot" (Piers Gaveston), having been murdered by the barons, had been laid to rest in the Church of the Dominicans. His son, Edward III, had created a hunting lodge, making a bathhouse built in 1368-69 known as "Les Stues". Richard only came there occasionally for the hunting or to keep Lent in the Dominican priory endowed by Edward. He had a strong inclination for the place because Richard's elder brother had been buried in a tomb there. The King commissioned some building at Langley, enlarging and embellishing the bathhouse and building, during the winter of 1386, chambers for de Vere and Mowbray. He created a Queen's garden, like the one at Sheen, but Langley was on a smaller scale than the other palaces. About two years later, two new timbered houses were completed, and another chamber for his friend the Earl of Stafford.[22] After Richard's murder at Pontefract, his body was borne to Langley to be first buried there.

During the middle 1390s, Richard had a new palace built, Windsor Manor, situated in the park, about five miles from Windsor Castle. According to the *King's Works*,[23] the King spent as much as £1,164 on the venture. The accomplished Court artist, Thomas Prince of Litlington, who lived in Cripplegate, was employed in painting its walls. Perhaps Richard intended Windsor Palace to be the main residence of his child-Queen Isabelle, for the disconsolate little girl was left there when her husband left on his second expedition to Ireland in 1399. If the building had been completed, it might have rivalled Sheen or Eltham in beauty.

After his painful experiences in the Tower, one might think that Richard would prefer not to live there ever again, but during the 1390s we find him decorating the fortress as a royal residence. He spent fairly lavishly on ornament in 1398, commissioning 105 square feet of painted glass, edged with *fleur-de-lis* and bordered by the royal arms. The Byward Tower, which still stands today, boasts rare wall paintings of the fourteenth century, well preserved considering their age, with their rich blues, gold, vermilion and *fleur-de-lis*.[24] The floor tiles bear leopards and Richard's badge of the White Hart. Dr. Tristam in his *English Wall Paintings of the Fourteenth Century* discusses the discoveries made in 1953.

Westminster is, however, Richard's crowning glory, especially the exquisite Westminster Hall, originally built in the reign of William Rufus, and rebuilt by Richard. Other kings such as Henry III, Edward II and Edward III had spent large sums making it beautiful but Richard wanted to give it grandeur also. The King may be justly accused of extravagance in many respects, but to charge him with profligacy in his paying out of £12,304 at Westminster, which included the expenses for the Coronation of Queen Isabelle, in his final years is hardly justified.

How much more beautiful Westminster Hall with its hammer beam roof must have appeared on completion than it does today! It was on November 3rd 1393 that the great architect Henry Yevele, famous for his work in the Abbey nave and at Canterbury, in collaboration with the carpenter Hugh Herland, was employed on this work. It must be remembered that there was not only a great Palace at Westminster, but a Privy Palace and a Prince's Palace. Westminster, in Richard's time, was the centre of administration, containing the Exchequer in its two-storeyed building and the Courts of Justice, the Court of Common Pleas and the King's Bench. The White Hall, so often mentioned in late fourteenth century chronicles, was a high-timbered building. One recalls Richard Fitzalan, Earl of Arundel, at bay before his judges in 1397 and Richard's vengeful cry: "Didst thou not say to me in the bath behind the White Hall that Sir Simon Burley, my Knight, was worthy of death?" If one were to try mentally to reconstruct Richard's Westminster, one must visualize the Great Hall of the Palace, the Little Hall and the Marculph Chamber, gay with paintings.

Richard possessed a deep veneration for Edward the Confessor, and during 1385, commissioned thirteen stone statues of Kings for the Palace, representing the Confessor and his twelve successors. He adopted his arms as his own, and commissioned two more statues, thought to represent that Saxon king and himself. Then he built a new great gateway to the Palace, embellishing it with a campanile and marble pillars.

Most of the best architects, artists, poets and writers, sculptors and others depended on the impeccable taste of King Richard and his uncle John of Gaunt. There are the glories of William of Wykeham's twin foundations of New College, Oxford, and of Winchester College. Who can fail to wax eloquent when viewing for the first time the fine gateway of Winchester College or the exquisite New College chapel (1383)? A Virgin at Winchester is a fine example of the stained medieval glass of Richard II's reign. It is the work of Thomas Glazier of Oxford. That epoch was truly splendid for much magnificent ecclesiastical architecture.

Bodiam Castle (1386), built for Sir Edward Dalyngridge, Knight of the Shire for Sussex, and closely associated with Richard's Court, is characteristic of the castles erected then. It was built on a quadrangular plan with a moat large enough to contain rooms looking out on a courtyard, a vision of medieval beauty, grandeur and enchantment. Other typical castles are Lumley in Durham completed by Ralph Lord Lumley in 1392, and Wardour in Wiltshire, built by John Lovell a year later.

Warkworth Castle in Northumberland, "this worm-eaten hold of ragged stone",[25] the ancient Seat of the Percies, stands in a magnificent position above the sweet river Coquet. It has strange memories of Henry, the first Percy Earl, and of Hotspur his son, whose lives were linked with Richard and his cousin, who usurped his throne.

There is further evidence of Richard's literary and artistic interests and his eager delight in elaborate book illustration in his personal manuscripts in the Bodleian Library, Oxford. Richard's Book of Divinations, known as *The Libellus Geomancie*, so lovingly preserved, is like an exquisite rare jewel. If Bodley MS.581 was prepared for the consolation of the King in March 1391 - fairly early during his personal rule - it certainly gives pleasure today, but it is for the scholar rather than the amateur. One must remember that books in Richard's day were manuscripts copied by hand and bound. Elegantly written in Latin in a beautiful script, they reveal Richard's interest in the metaphysical, the interpretation of dreams, and a liking for astrology. The King was certainly superstitious and Gervase Mathew points outs that folio 87 in the King's 'Rosarium Regis Ricardi' (his Rosary) purports to ask a series of questions regarding the fidelity of the King's friends, the strength of Chastity and so forth. It is fascinating to conjecture whether Richard used it during critical phases of his reign to ascertain whether a man was true or false. Folio 9 is the King himself at the age of 24, a handsome man without a beard, dressed in blue, wearing a crown on his head. Another depicts a man in pink, riding a horse against a chequered background of blue and pink, and of one in a russet suit bearing a dagger.

The great Bible of Richard II is today in the British Library[26] with the inscription "Omnia leuia sunt amanti" ('all things are light to the lover'). Another curious manuscript in Richard's library is *The Book against the twelve errors and heresies of the Lollards*[27] by the Court Dominican Roger Dymoke, perhaps commissioned by Richard II, himself an orthodox Catholic. Queen's College Oxford possesses a letter of Richard's first Queen, Anne, written in 1384 on the subject of learning.[28]

It is written to my "most dere sovereign lord and husband". Richard and Anne were no doubt particularly interested in Queen's College because it had reputedly been founded by Richard's grandmother, Philippa of Hainault, though in reality it was founded by her Chaplain in her honour. When the provost Thomas Carlisle, a considerable benefactor, appealed to the King, he took over the interests of the College, committing its custody to the Chancellor and Treasurer of England and other officials.

Anne wrote:

> Please hit your grace to wytt that where as our Queen Philippe sometime Quene of England of famous memory ffounded a college in the University of Oxfford called the Quenes College to have perpetually within the said college at the leste nombre on provoste XII scolers off the same college ffour chaplens and two maistris. Off the children beynge scolers . . . oon of them to instruct and informe scolers in the facute of art and the oder of them to instruct and informe scolers in their gramer . . . to pray syng and saye divine service.

The King was requested to grant his precious letters patent "under the grete sele". This led to successive kings of England assuming the protection and interests of the College.

In his early literary career, John Gower owed much to the patronage of King Richard. In the first edition of his work *The*

94

Confessio Amantis, he relates how it came about that he wrote "a boke for Kinge Rychardes sake".

> To whom belongeth my ligeance
> With all my hartes obeysance
> with all that ener a lyege may done or do.

He was rowing on the Thames one day when by chance he met the King in his barge.

> he bad me come into his barge
> and when I was with him at large
> he hath this charge upon me leyde
> and bad me do my busynesse
> Some newe things I should boke.[29]

However, Gower bore the King little gratitude, for he soon became disillusioned with Richard's autocratic government. By 1393, he was ready to transfer his allegiance to the Earl of Derby, the King's cousin. He admired Henry as a gallant knight and for his grace. There is no reference whatsoever to Richard in a new edition of *The Confessio Amantis*. Instead, the slightly grovelling lines:

> I sende unto myn owne lorde
> which of Lancastre is Henry named.

In return, Gower received an annual grant of two pipes of Gascon wine after Henry IV ascended the throne.

Scholars today are of the opinion that one of the best illustrations in *The Confessio Amantis* is by Herman Scheere, from Cologne, an artist at Richard's Court. The richness and delicacy of the houpelande worn by the lover are characteristic of his work.

Gower wrote in several languages, including English and Latin and he was cosmopolitan in his outlook. In the first book of *The Vox Clamantis* written in Latin, he attacks the peasants at the time of the Rising, calling them lustful because they coveted what they did not own. Their lust had turned them into beasts. However, in the later books of this work, for instance in the 'Epistula', he turns his attack on Richard and his counsellors. Gower was of independent means, unlike most of the contemporary poets such as Thomas Hoccleve, so he never spared those he condemned. His work had a wide appeal in his own day, and *The Confessio Amantis* was translated into Castilian and Portuguese.[30]

The great Geoffrey Chaucer had several patrons: Richard II, John of Gaunt, the Countess of March and possibly Robert de Vere. The daily pitcher of wine allowed him by Edward III in 1374 became, under King Richard, an annual tun. His first masterpiece *Troilus and Griseyde* seems to have offended Queen Anne because it implies that women were more faithless than men. Therefore, as a penance, she commanded him to write *The Legend of Gode Women*.

> Be ye my guide my lady sovereign
> As to my earthly god to you I call,
> Both in this work, as in my sorrowes all.

It may well be that his allegorical poem *The Assembly of Foules*, usually assumed to be a reference to the first marriage of John of Gaunt with the Lady Blanche of Lancaster, was in reality written to celebrate Richard's marriage with Anne. Parts of *The Canterbury Tales* were composed during Richard's reign, probably between 1387 and 1388. It is curious that Chaucer's name is derived from the French "chaussier", suggesting that his family were once shoemakers, but his father and grandfather, in fact, were both wine merchants.[31]

Chaucer was not only a courtier but was employed as a secretary in the diplomatic service in its very early days. He accompanied Sir Thomas Percy to Flanders in 1377 and he travelled in Italy. His family connection with the Courts of Edward III and Richard II was very intimate because his wife Philippa was bedchamber woman to Blanche of Lancaster at the Savoy Palace, while his sister-in-law Katherine Swynford,[32] a woman of considerable character and tact, was governess to John of Gaunt's legitimate children and for many years his mistress. *The Book of the Duchess*, an early work, was inspired by the death of Blanche in 1369, beloved as she was by everybody.

It was the fashion at Richard's Court for poems on the theme of courtly love to be read aloud to the courtiers and their ladies as they indolently indulged themselves in the gardens of his palaces on a summer day or strolled in the avenues. Chaucer, clad in pink, would read from a pulpit from his *Troilus and Griseyde* or from the translation of the *Roman de la Rose*. In the winter months, the storytelling and recital of poetry would take place between vespers - about 3 p.m. - and the supper of wine and spiced cakes that followed. Richard continued his patronage of Chaucer until the end of his reign, arranging for the poet to be paid £10 every six months. Henry IV presented Chaucer with a scarlet robe trimmed with fur and confirmed his cousin's grants, adding forty marks of his own. Chaucer's *Compleynt of Mars* is supposed to allude to the love of Richard's half-brother Sir John Holland (Earl of Huntingdon) for Isabella, Duchess of York, notorious for her love affairs.

Thomas Hoccleve, a younger contemporary of Thomas Usk (executed in 1388), is a highly original but rather underrated poet. He prided himself on being a personal disciple of Chaucer, writing of him "my worthy maister Chaucer, the first fynder of our faire language". He was a year or so younger than King Richard, and among his political poems is a morbid ballade (a poem of one or more triplets of seven-level or eight-lined stanzas) after Richard's bones were brought to Westminster from Langley. As Hoccleve was an obscure clerk in the Privy Office, it is unlikely that he enjoyed an intimate relationship with Chaucer, the friend of royalty.[33] The "father of English poetry" was already dead by 1400, while Hoccleve lived probably for another thirty years.

The autobiographical element in his work is so marked that we know quite a lot about him. In his wild, lustful youth, Hoccleve was most at home in the taverns and cook-houses of Richard II's London, making love to the flirtatious, lusty girls in the 'Paul's Head' Tavern. Perhaps he was a little boastful, wanting his readers to think him a very devil. He drank harder than any of his colleagues in the Privy Office,[34] but he tells us that when he haunted the taverns

> Had I a kus (kiss) I was content ful weel,
> Bettre than I wolde be with the deed.

However, he could never resist Bacchus and his lure. Though never fortunate enough to enjoy financial security and often in debt, he was generous with his money, being dubbed "a verray gentil man" in the Westminster cook-shops. He was flattered when called "maister" by the London watermen.

Hoccleve tells us that he once met an old man in the Strand, who advised him how to make money.

> Sharpe thy penne and write on lustily
> Lete see, my son, make it fresshe and gay
> Uttre thyne art as thou canst, craftily.

Good advice for a writer, even today! His magnum opus was *The Regimen of Princes*,[35] a didactic poem, dedicated to Prince Hal, the future Henry V.

Another Court poet was John Lydgate, possible author of *London Lickpenny*, and influenced during his early career by Chaucer. He really belongs to a later era since he was only just beginning to write during the 1390s. Like Hoccleve, he greatly esteemed Chaucer, relating how "he first distilled the golde dewedropes of speche and eloquence into our tunge". In Lydgate's major poems such as *Temple of Glas*, he reveals his gift for language.

Will Langland as a poet was essentially a prophet, too proud by nature to serve or flatter a patron. His sympathies are with the poor and downtrodden, so he writes of the misery and monotony of their lives with a terrible despair. Not for him the generous humanity of Chaucer or his all-pervading sympathy. He had an intimate knowledge of the London of Richard II, describing the strange characters he encountered, such as a ribidor (a rebeck player), a rationer (a rat catcher) and a raker of Chepe (a Cheapside scavenger).

The loveliest work of art during Richard's reign is undoubtedly the celebrated Wilton Diptych, formerly owned by the Earl of Pembroke at Wilton House and in Charles I's collection. Today it can be seen in the National Gallery. Its sacred beauty glows in the memory. One is thankful that it has never been restored, unlike the splendid, contemporary portrait of Richard II in his Coronation robes attributed to a French artist, André Beauneveu of the

98

Court of Charles VI, known to have visited Richard's Court in the 1390s. Today it hangs in the nave of Westminster Abbey, much admired by visitors. Two experts, the late Dr. P. Tancred Borenius and Dr. Tristam, consider that it was painted in 1390 when the King was twenty-three. Is it possible, however, that it is the work of a Bohemian Court painter who had come over earlier with Anne of Bohemia?

In the Wilton Diptych, the young King Richard is wearing a dress of gold tissue decorated with medallions of the hart. He is kneeling in an attitude of reverence before the Virgin, attended by two Kings, Edmund the Martyr and Edward the Confessor, while his patron saint, John the Baptist, lays his protective hand on Richard's shoulder. Dr. Joan Evans suggests that the Wilton Diptych must have been painted in England, and may have been the work of an English artist. However, the whole conception of the work is French. In contemporary France there were many pictures of great men and their patron saints kneeling before the Virgin. Such an example is in a manuscript in the Brussels Royal Library, where the Duc de Berry and St. John are shown kneeling before the Virgin and Child. It is fascinating to speculate whether the Wilton Diptych was Richard's personal possession, possibly a portable altar. There are paintings on the back, too, depicting his coat of arms.

The subject of this exquisite work is controversial. Gervase Mathew thinks that it represents Richard's Coronation, in his eleventh year, since there are eleven angels in blue dresses round the Virgin, in a part of the panel. However, the use of Richard's device of the white hart on his own dress and that of the angels, first adopted by the King in 1390, suggests the date is about 1395, when Anglo-French negotiations were being pursued. It could portray Richard vowing to lead a crusade at this period when a joint crusading expedition was under serious consideration.[36]

Gervase Mathew suggests that the white hart of the Wilton Diptych was painted by John Siferwas, a brilliant artist of that period. If born about 1360, he would have been thirty-five when he painted the white hart. Siferwas came of a knightly Hereford-shire family, and he was head of a fashionable *atelier*. His brilliant portrait of birds is intensely individual and alive, and can be seen in an artist's sketch book in Magdalene College, Cambridge (Pepys Collection). The names of the patrons of this gifted artist are known: Richard Medford (Richard II's Secretary from 1385 to 1395, an intimate friend and later Bishop of Salisbury), John Lord Lovell, and Robert Bruynyng, for thirty years Abbot of Sherborne. Whether or not Siferwas painted the White Hart of the Wilton Diptych one can only speculate, but he was responsible for the Sherborne Missal with its crucifixion scene, another great work.

VIII   Richard in Ireland

During Richard's personal rule in May 1392, he again quarrelled with the City of London. His Court was both expensive and difficult to maintain without constant recourse to moneylenders. The Londoners not only refused to grant the King a loan of £1,000, but attacked a Lombard merchant who agreed to do so.[1] While it was an act of folly to antagonize the City, the Londoners' shameful treatment of the Lombard merchant was also open to censure. Clearly, Richard had not forgiven the City for siding with the Lords Appellant during 1387-88. There were rights and wrongs on both sides. Higden, the contemporary Chronicler, is very critical, attacking the Londoners as "greedy, arrogant and turbulent folks, these supporters of Lollardy and contemners of God and the ancient traditions".[2]

Yet the King must be blamed for his arbitrary acts in sequestrating the ancient liberties of the City of London and deposing the mayor John Hende, putting in his place as Warden a Knight of Sussex, Sir Edward Dalyngridge. He even imprisoned Hende and two sheriffs, ordering Sir Edward Dalyngridge to govern London in Hende's place. To show his grave displeasure, he ordered that the royal Courts should be removed from London to York.[3] It is evident that Richard wanted to humiliate the Londoners, to lessen the risks of a City rising and to force the citizens to plead in a strange place.

While we must not condone the King's actions, they are surely understandable when we consider the continual state of violence that prevailed then. A typical incident occurred in 1392 when a baker's man with a basket of "horse-bread" came to serve his master's customers in Salisbury Alley, Fleet Street, and was attacked by a servant of John Waltham, Bishop of Salisbury, whose sympathies lay with the Court party. An ancient Chronicle tells the whole story,[4] "and he tok an horsloff out of the basket of the baker; and he askyd 'whi he dede so' . . . and he brak from ham and fledde yn

- to the lordes - place." The Bishop of Salisbury complained of the behaviour of the people of London to Thomas Arundel, Archbishop of York, and then Chancellor of England.[5]

In their predicament, the citizens of London were forced to buy their pardon from Richard for £10,000 and to pay a special fine of £3,000.

To obtain his forgiveness was no easy matter. Knowing of the King's love for pageantry and his marked theatrical sense, the City Companies and aldermen staged an elaborate show. When the King and Queen rode through the City down Cheap one August day, they found the streets bedecked with gold and silver tissue and decorated with tapestries. Costly presents were showered on Richard and Anne.

> And whanne the King come to the gate of the Brygge of London, here they presentid hym with a mylke-white stede, sadelled and brydilled, and trapped with white cloth of golde and red parted togadir, and the Quene a palfraye alle white trappid yn the same aray with white and rede, and the condites of London Ronnen white wyne and rede, for all maner pepill to drynke of.[6]

At Temple Bar, a splendid Tableau depicting the King's special saint, John the Baptist, was given in his honour.

Richard of Maidstone, John of Gaunt's confessor, relates that Queen Anne fell on her knees before her husband to intercede for the citizens in Westminster Hall. Thus she addressed him: "My King, my husband, my light, my life! Sweet love, without whose life mine would be but death." Then the King raised the Queen to sit on his throne and granted all her wishes. It is said also that John of Gaunt, with other "worthi lordes and ladies" intervened on behalf of the citizens of London.

So the King decided to pardon the City magnates, remitting some of the fines and allowing the Courts of Common Pleas, the Chancery and Exchequer to return to Westminster from York. One wonders, however, whether the King was aware of the dangerous resentment brooding in the minds of the civic authorities and indeed among the Londoners. They were never to forgive him. In

102

judging his actions one must always remember that Richard was consistent in one thing. He was always a medieval king and never a democrat.

According to the Monk of Westminster the King kept Christmas that year (1392-93) at Eltham. The Londoners, still eager to appease Richard, sent mummers to entertain the King and Queen. When they waited upon him in great state about Epiphany (January 6th) they presented him with a dromedary, a one-humped camel for riding. To the Queen they gave "a large and remarkable bird" with an enormously wide throat (gullet), perhaps a pelican.

During the early years of Richard's personal rule, Henry Bolingbroke thought it politic, probably on the advice of his father, to keep out of the way, and undertook two crusading expeditions to Prussia, travel in Lithuania and a pilgrimage to Jerusalem (1391-93). His uncle Gloucester also set out for Prussia in 1391, but was forced to abandon the expedition owing to bad weather. On this occasion the Duke of Gloucester presented to the Church of St. Peter (Westminster Abbey) a magnificent vestment of cloth of gold, red in colour, with orphreys of black velvet embroidered with the capital letters T A ('T' and 'A', the initial letters of Thomas of Woodstock and his wife Alianore [Eleanor]). The swans, the device on the Bohun badge, skilfully stitched to the vestment, enhanced its beauty. Unfortunately, Gloucester's relations with the Abbey became very cool later on and he subsequently took these gifts back.

Gloucester, during 1389, had been appointed Justice of Chester and in the following year, Justice for life. However, when a rebellion broke out in Cheshire four years later, the Earl of Arundel, who was then residing in Lion Castle at Holt, on the River Dee - for he owned estates on the borders of Cheshire - did absolutely nothing to quell the revolt. Nor did Gloucester. The revolt had actually been inflamed by the grievances of soldiers and others returned from the wars, many of them unemployed and unemployable, only too ready to resent the policy of peace with France, advocated by the King and John of Gaunt. The causes for the trouble were economic rather than political.

The situation became so critical that Richard was obliged to summon back his uncle the Duke of Lancaster from his peacemaking mission in France. Gaunt showed statesmanship and firmness in pacifying the rebels, having the good sense to provide work for the malcontents by enrolling them for service in his new Duchy of Aquitaine. A merciful policy was adopted towards the ringleaders, though Richard was later accused of leniency and partiality when reappointing his friend Sir Thomas Talbot, leader of the Cheshire rebels, a King's Knight after a brief spell in the Tower. After the Cheshire Rising, it was galling for Gloucester to be removed from his life appointment as Justice of Cheshire and North Wales. He was replaced by Mowbray, Earl of Nottingham.

The fiery Earl of Arundel's character had mellowed - at least temporarily - by 1394, possibly influenced by his infatuation for his new young wife, Philippa Hastings, a granddaughter of Lionel, Duke of Clarence. He gave her lavish presents. By now he was aged forty-seven, in that age considered almost elderly.

When Parliament assembled in January, however, Gaunt accused Arundel of conniving with the Cheshire rebels.[7] The infuriated Arundel then turned on the King's uncle, full of rancour and hatred because he was so high in Richard's favour. His strong personal attack on the Duke of Lancaster in fact implied an attack on the King. It was contrary to Richard's honour that he should be seen constantly walking arm-in-arm with his uncle, and that he should wear the collar of the Lancastrian livery, a course followed by his retainers. He accused Gaunt of using such "rough and bitter words" both in Council and in Parliament that he, the Earl and others often dared not declare their views or intentions. He complained that the title of Duke of Guyenne had been given to Lancaster. It was greatly to the King's disadvantage that he had granted his uncle the Duchy of Aquitaine. Clearly, Arundel wanted to revive the King's former suspicions against his uncle, but he completely failed to take into account the changed conditions. Gaunt was now a respected elder statesman.

Richard replied in detail to Arundel's accusations. If he walked arm-in-arm with Lancaster, so did he habitually with his other uncles also. As for the livery, in point of fact, on John of Gaunt's return from Spain he had himself taken the collar from his uncle's neck, pleased to wear it "en signe de bon amour d'entier cor entre eux".[8] He had told his retainers to do likewise. He denied that

Lancaster had ever overborne any member of his Council in his hearing. The grant of the Duchy of Guyenne had been made with the full consent of Parliament. As for the cost of the army in Spain, 200,000 marks had been freely voted.

Arundel received no support for his attack on Gaunt, and the King demanded a public apology. The Rolls of Parliament mention his words:

> Sire, sith that hit seemeth to the Kyng and to the other lordes, and eke that yhe been so mychel greved and displesid be my wordes, hit forthynketh me, and bysech youe of your gude lordship to remyt me your mautalent.[9]

> (Sire, since it seems to the King and to the other lords, and also that ye be so much grieved and displeased by my words, it seems to me and I beseech you of your good lordship to remove from me your displeasure.)

What rankled most with Arundel was the Duke of Lancaster's peace mission in France.

1394 was a fatal year for royal deaths. During March there died John of Gaunt's second wife, Constanza of Castile, who had always been so Spanish in her adopted country. Gaunt had never cared for her. For many years after the death of the enchanting Blanche, his mistress Lady Katherine Swynford had held the first place in his heart. She was not only extremely attractive but she possessed a brilliant personality. Her great tact ensured her an honoured place at Court. The Duke of Lancaster, however, was determined to give Constanza a magnificent funeral. So he lavished the large sum of £584 5s. 9½d. on her funeral in the Collegiate Church of Our Lady in the Newark at Leicester [10] and provided in his will that a chantry be built there to pray for his soul and Dame Constanza for ever.

Three months later there died at Sheen Richard's beloved Queen Anne, aged twenty-eight. It occurred on Whit Sunday, June 7th. The probable cause of her death was 'the plague'. The King was grief-stricken. How cruel and inexorable was fate to deprive Richard of his Anne! If she had lived, is it possible that her beneficial influence might have restrained him from his worst excesses, such as forced loans, and his fatal mistake in confiscating the Lancastrian estates of the cousin who was to usurp his throne?

So that the funeral might be as magnificent as possible it was postponed until August 3rd. Queen Anne's body first lay in state in St. Paul's, then was borne in procession to the burial place in Westminster Abbey. Among the Abbey manuscripts are the expenses incurred by Peter Combe, the sacrist for wax "and about the making of tapers square and round for Queen Anne".[11] *The Brut Chronicle*[12] mentions that "she was beryed and worthily entered besyde Saint Edwardes Shryne; on whose soule Almyhti God have mercy and pite! amen!" All the peers attended the obsequies, and arrived punctually except for the tactless Richard Fitzalan, Earl of Arundel, who went out of his way to insult his enemy the King, probably by way of revenge for his humiliation in Parliament during January. A terrible incident marred the proceedings. When Arundel at last arrived and during the service asked the King to excuse his attendance "for certain urgent private reasons", Richard completely lost control of himself. Seizing a wand from one of the vergers, he struck him with such violence on his head that he fell to the ground, while blood oozed from his wound on the sacred precincts of the Abbey.

The Cambridge Medieval History relates: "His passionate grief at the death of Queen Anne in 1394 and his violence in striking Arundel to the ground in Westminster Abbey showed his old unbalanced temperament." True enough, Richard must be blamed for his violent temper in this sacred place, but the work makes no mention of the provocation the King had received from the nobleman. Arundel's insolent bearing and behaviour in the Abbey caused Richard's outburst. He was arrested and imprisoned in the Tower for a week before being released.

The tomb of Richard and Anne is in St. Edward's Chapel. It is fitting that their effigies should lie together thus, their hands linked, united in death as they had been in life. The monument was begun in 1395 and was completed two years later at a cost of £400 by Nicholas Broker and Godfrey Prest of Wood Street. Later, Richard granted Abbot William Colchester and the Prior and Convent of Westminster £200 per annum to provide an anniversary for himself and his late Queen.[13]

After her death, the King, crazed with grief, passionately mourned the death of his dearest companion. She was the lodestar of his Court, the sharer in all his artistic enterprises. He ordered John Gedney, Clerk of Works to demolish to the ground not only La Neyt, the island sanctuary, but also the entire Palace of Sheen. When one considers Richard's emotional nature such a drastic act is completely understandable. It is a false conclusion, however, to think of Richard as extremely neurotic after her death or as suffering from schizophrenia. In many respects he showed a ripe political judgement, an almost uncanny insight in dealing with his suspected enemies.

It is an intriguing question as to whether it was Richard or Anne who was responsible for their childless marriage, but it is impossible to determine. Richard had a double, a favourite clerk named Richard Maudelyn, reputed to bear a strong resemblance to him and even to be an illegitimate son, but this is probably legend. What is clear is that the royal widower, at the age of twenty-seven, faced an almost intolerable burden.

By a strange coincidence, there also died during July, Mary de Bohun, Countess of Derby, Henry Bolingbroke's wife. She was only twenty-four, a musical, gentle woman, who had given Henry six children, including his eldest son Henry (the future Henry V) born at Monmouth Castle (1387).

For some time before the decease of Queen Anne, the King had been planning an expedition to Ireland. He owed his title of 'Seigneur d'Ireland' or 'Lord of Ireland' to Henry II, a title conferred by this ruthless King on his youngest son, John.[14] By implication a feudal title, it remained the style of the English Crown over Ireland till 1541 (during Henry VIII's reign). During Richard's reign, Ireland was in a state of anarchy, having been neglected by previous rulers too preoccupied with other affairs. Ireland was an increasing burden on the English Exchequer, for the cost of administration amounted to £20,000 per annum: and no income now came from the annual revenue of the Irish Exchequer.

So, the King's object in visiting his 'Lordship in Ireland' during the autumn of 1394 was partly political and partly economic. Above all, he wanted to define the legal relations of the Gaelic kings with the English Crown.[15] There are a number of notarial deeds and documents in the Public Record Office showing how the

Irish chiefs submitted to their overlord, the King of England. Richard, always keenly interested in Ireland, intended to restore efficiency and order to the decaying Anglo-Irish government. He showed genuine statesmanship in his Irish policy, deeply sincere in his efforts to conciliate the Irish leaders and to find a solution to a problem still troubling statesmen six centuries later.

His first move was to order the absentee Irish living in England to return to Ireland.[16] When writing to his uncle Edmund, Duke of York, on February 1st 1395 - Richard had created Edmund, Regent, while he was absent from the Kingdom - he mentions three categories of Irishmen: 'the wild Irish, our enemies', the Irish rebels (the degenerate English) and the obedient English.

Sailing from Haverford West, the royal party reached Waterford on October 2nd 1394. Richard was accompanied by four great lords - his cousin Roger Mortimer, Earl of March and Ulster, heir presumptive to the throne and owner of vast Irish estates; his half-brother John Holland; Thomas Mowbray, Earl of Nottingham, Marshal of England; and Richard's new favourite, Edward Earl of Rutland, recently created Earl of Cork. In one of his letters,[17] the King refers to the late arrival of his uncle the Duke of Gloucester. Among others accompanying Richard were Sir Thomas Percy, Seneschal and Marshal of the Household, and Thomas Merke, later Bishop of Carlisle, a loyal friend. According to Henry Crystede, a squire of King Richard's, in his later account to Jean Froissart in England, Richard had with him at least four thousand knights and squires and thirty thousand archers, "all of whom were well and punctually paid week by week". Ireland was then a strange, wild country, consisting of tall forests, great stretches of water, bogs and uninhabitable regions very difficult to subdue. He described the Irish as "hard people and of rude engine and wit".

Richard II's letters during his eight months in Ireland are of much interest. They have been edited and translated by the late Dr. Edmund Curtis.[18] Letter I is written to Thomas Arundel, Archbishop of York, Chancellor of England:

> Very reverend Father in God, we greet you with all our heart, and would have you know that, as regards ourselves, our well-being and estate, we had the finest and most favourable cros-

108

sing, with full health of body, without being troubled or upset by the weather or rough sea in any way . . . we were only
a day and a night at sea in our crossing; and so we arrived at
our city of Waterford . . . where we have found victuals in
great plenty and very cheap, and where from one day to
another our loyal lieges come in to offer us their services
against every design of the others who have been rebels and
adversaries to us in our absence . . .

On October 19th he relates to Arundel how he lodged at Jerpoint
where he heard of the arrival "of our very dear uncle at Waterford". He met the Duke of Gloucester in the wood of Leglin.
Richard tells his Chancellor how he dislodged several of his enemies including the MacMurroughs, burning their houses. Art Oge
MacMurrough, King of Leinster, an expert in guerrilla fighting,
cunningly contrived to conceal his men in woods and mountains,
trying to hold up the English advancing from Waterford to Dublin.
There were no pitched battles. Richard, in his letters, mentions
how his former adversaries Anolam O'Nolan and his son Shane,

came to make obeisance to us, bare-headed, disarmed, their
girdles undone, holding their swords by the points with the
pommels erect, and put themselves unreservedly (*de haut en
bas*) at our mercy without any conditions.[18]

After burning the lands of the MacMurroughs, Richard made
them swear an oath on the Cross of Dublin "to be our faithful and
loyal subjects". When O'Byrne, O'Toole and Shane O'Nolan accompanied the King to Dublin, "moved by pity, we received them
into our grace".

The King, too trusting, had, perhaps unwisely, released the
MacMurroughs after their capture. He relates how valiantly his
cousin, the Earl of Rutland, fought against them, capturing 8,000
cattle of the MacMurroughs. On one occasion, Rutland nearly sur-
prised the Irish chief while he was in bed with his wife. Richard,
always interested in dress, describes how a coffer was found be-
longing to MacMurrough's wife in which were various articles of
feminine use but of no great value.

In a letter to the Duke of York, his uncle, whom Richard had appointed Regent in England, he tells him how his son Edward had fought a battle at Munster in which he had gained a victory.

The King rewarded his entourage with large grants of land, among them Janico d'Artas (or "of Artois"), a favourite squire of Richard's, who may have served in the wars in Gascony.

Janico wrote proudly to Richard Medford, Bishop of Salisbury, Treasurer of England, to tell him that the King had granted him a parcel of land (1395) in the country of the Irish rebels (Leinster), "which if it were in the parts of London would be worth by the year fifty thousand marks".[19] We hear of Janico again on Richard's second expedition to Ireland (1399) doing yeoman service.

Froissart relates how useful James Butler, Earl of Ormond was to the King, particularly because of his fluent command of the Gaelic language. Because of this, he was commissioned to negotiate with the chiefs of Munster, once subdued, and the country about the Shannon. His patient skill in diplomacy was responsible for bringing to terms Brian O'Brien, son of Mahon King of Thomond, great Irish landowners since the thirteenth century. Brian wrote to King Richard: "Among all the English and Irish I have acquired neither lands nor possessions by conquest nor any profit save as your ancestors gave to mine." When Richard's uncle, Lionel of Clarence, was in Ireland, he and his father had been foremost in offering him fealty and honour. Now he hastened to do likewise in offering Richard homage in St. Thomas's Abbey in Dublin.

What a triumph for the King in Dublin when eighty Irish chiefs, speaking Irish, paid homage to "the lord of Ireland", while Ormond and other Anglo-Irish assisted as interpreters. Crystede related to Froissart how four Irish Kings were entertained by Richard. Froissart described them as uncouth. He related most amusingly how they were taught the civilized manners of Richard's Court. As their tutor, the King appointed his squire Crystede. He possessed admirable qualifications: not only did he speak Gaelic but he was also bilingual in English and French. As the Irish kings did not wear breeches, Crystede arranged for a large number of linen drawers to be made and sent to them. Instead of Irish cloaks, they were advised to wear robes trimmed with miniver and squirrel, strange as such rich garments might seem to them. Again, they were introduced to saddles and stirrups on horseback. Since their table manners were boorish, Crystede arranged for them to eat from individual drinking vessels and dishes. All these things were necessary before they could be considered worthy of the honour of knighthood.

Richard's first expedition to Ireland was a resounding success, and the enormous expense involved well justified. His policy of pacification and appeasement certainly paid dividends, as did the creation of 'English land', with the further introduction of English colonists.[20] It was also a clever diplomatic move to have the banners of his royal arms impaled with those of the greatly revered Edward the Confessor. This King was also venerated in Ireland because the Irish hated the Danes knowing that the Confessor, once their conqueror, had been driven from his Kingdom by their machinations. When Gloucester returned to England during 1395, he had no difficulty whatever in obtaining further funds from a Parliament warmly appreciative of the work accomplished. It was deeply unfortunate, however, that the King could not stay longer in Ireland as he had wanted to, for during that winter he received pressing, and then more urgent, messages that his presence was required in London. The Council, particularly Archbishop Arundel of York and Bishop Braybrook of London, were deeply troubled by the activities of the 'Lollards'. In a document placed before Parliament they advocated a complete reform of the Church and were deeply critical of the luxurious dresses and ornaments worn at Court. They were pacifists, like the later Quakers. To overcome Richard's reluctance to leave Ireland, Arundel and Braybrook interviewed him there. By his intelligent diplomacy the King might have achieved a lasting peace if he could have remained there longer.

One Irish chief, O'Neill, wrote in great distress when Richard was about to depart: "It is openly foretold that after your departure my lord the Earl of Ulster will wage bitter war against you." Actually Roger Mortimer, the King's deputy, spent two years in trying to recover his earldom. Nevertheless, to complete the pacification would have entailed the appointment of a series of impartial viceroys.

Richard departed from Waterford on May 15th in his ship *The Trinity*, taking with him various deeds and indentures recording the submissions of eighty Irish chiefs. Other troubles immediately confronted him at home. It is evident that Richard, a devout and orthodox Catholic, had no sympathy whatever for the Lollards, but he was humane, disliking the persecution of the heretics. What exasperated him was the knowledge that prominent members of his Court were active Lollards, such as Sir Richard Stury,[21] Sir Lewis Clifford and Lord John Montague, brother of the Earl of Salisbury (himself a Lollard). He now flew into one of his violent rages, threatening Stury that unless he refrained from ever breaking the oath of recantation, he would meet with the foulest death that was possible. Stury's and Clifford's offence had been to present a bill in Parliament clamouring for reform of the Church. Their petition had been nailed to the doors of Westminster Abbey and St. Paul's, open to public inspection.

Yet Richard resisted the pressure of the Church authorities to inflict the ultimate sanction of burning the heretics at the stake. There was a lot of discussion by heresy-hunters as to the advisability of resorting to such a drastic and terrible punishment, probably introduced to frighten their opponents, and also by the Lollards in their appeals to Parliament to determine the matter in dispute. Yet the penalties invoked by the government were comparatively mild - imprisonment and confiscation of a man's goods.[22] If a former Lollard agreed to renounce his former heretical opinions and to refrain from reading any English books of Lollard origin, he was usually released from confinement. Such an offender was John Croft, who appeared before the King at Windsor at the end of April 1397. He now asked for pardon, having renounced any heretical opinions he may have expressed.[23] Yet Richard must have shown considerable zeal, for Archbishop Arundel complimented the King for his support against the Lollards in 1396.

By temperament Richard's successor, Henry IV, was more prepared than his cousin to persecute to the death, almost certainly influenced by Archbishop Arundel, the archenemy of the Lollards. Consequently the infamous statute 'De Heretico Comburendo' was passed by Parliament (March 10th 1401), legalizing the ultimate sanction of burning at the stake for heretics. One of the first to

112

suffer was a brave man, William Sautre, a parish priest. Daring to defy Arundel on the subject of transubstantiation, he was burnt to death at Smithfield "chained standing to a post in a barrel, packed round with blazing faggots". Today we would rightly condemn both Henry and Arundel as monsters of cruelty and inhumanity, but it is fair to judge them by the standards of their own age, one of religious intolerance and persecution.

One great statute passed in 1393 during Richard's personal rule, that of 'Praemunire', steadfastly upheld the rights and independence of England in selecting her own archbishops, bishops, clergy and abbots, jealous of papal interference or encroachment on this privilege. Earlier statutes of like nature had received the sanction of Parliament during the reign of Edward III, Richard's grandfather, in 1351 and later, but Richard's statute clarified the position in no uncertain way:

> A Common clamor is made, that the said father the Pope both ordained and purposed to translate some prelates without the King's assent and knowledge, and without the assent of the prelates ... so the Crown of England, which hath been so free at all times, that it hath been in subjection to no realm, but immediately subject to God in all things touching the regality of the same Crown, and none other, should be submitted to the Pope ... if any purchase or pursue in the Court of Rome any such translations etc which touch the King Our Lord against him, his crown, and his regality or his realm ... that process be made against them by praemunire facias.[24]

It was natural for Richard and many of his advisers not only to detest the Lollards, but to be sensitive to Papal interference in the affairs of England.

It was Richard who first took the initiative to broach a possible marriage between himself and a princess of France whilst still in Ireland. At first, Isabelle, eldest daughter of Charles VI, was not even mentioned in his letter to the King of France.[25] Serious negotiations for Isabelle's hand only began during May 1395 after Richard had returned to England. A little girl not yet eight years of age was a curious choice for a widower of twenty-eight. It has often been said that Richard, after such a happy first marriage, could not bear to consummate a second marriage so soon after Anne's death. This may be true. However, the ostensible reason for the marriage was the King's desire for a long truce with France. The protracted negotiations for a permanent peace were proving difficult, owing to French intransigence concerning England's financial demands and her refusal to surrender Calais.

One eminent historian, Professor Tout, alleges that the King had a more sinister motive in embarking on his French marriage, hoping that his father-in-law Charles VI might help him to attain absolute power against his enemies at home. Certainly a curious phrase is contained in the negotiations for a final truce. The King of France and other members of the royal family "were to aid and sustain Richard with all their power against any of his subjects".[26] Yet, in his final extremity, when his enemies had him at their mercy, there is no evidence that Richard turned in desperation to Charles to save him.

At home the King's policy towards France was that of a peacemaker, for he understood before his time the utter illusory nature of war. In *The Correspondence of Richard II*, the King reveals a desire to foster other royal alliances, one between his friend the Earl of Rutland and Charles VI's second daughter and between Henry, eldest son of the Duke of Lancaster, and Michelle, Charles's youngest daughter.[27] Nothing, however, came of either proposed marriage.

His second marriage was not popular among the people and opposed by the fiery Gloucester and the war party. John of Gaunt was in charge of the negotiations, but Sir Thomas Percy and his brother, the Earl of Northumberland, both played a part.

Richard visited Calais twice before the final celebrations. They were on a magnificent scale, resembling the later Field of Cloth of Gold. The King was accompanied by the Duke of Lancaster, his son the Earl of Derby, and his other uncles, Gloucester and York. John of Gaunt had recently married his mistress Lady Katherine Swynford, much to the indignation of the Duchess of Gloucester and other high-born ladies. Despite their earlier protests, the new Duchess of Lancaster was to accompany Queen Isabelle to England in their company.

114

Each day King Richard wore different dresses, a long gown of red velvet, a headdress given to him by Charles VI of France studded with precious stones and on his breast the hart of his own livery. On the following day Richard donned a motely gown, of white and red velvet. In honour of the dead Queen Anne, the Lords were resplendent in red velvet gowns, with 'the bend' of the livery of Richard's first Queen. When the King was first presented to Isabelle by his father-in-law, he courteously took her by the hand making much of her, thanking the King of France for bestowing on him "such an honourable and beloved gift". The precocious Isabelle, having heard much of the beauties of Richard's palaces, was nothing loath to be Queen of England.

The Brut relates how she was brought to Saint Nicholas's Church in Calais, to be "worthily weddyd with the most solemnite . . . and alle mynystries of holy Churche".[28] All kinds of delicacies and rare wines were consumed at the ensuing royal banquet.

It is difficult to extinguish enmity between two countries after long years of warfare. While the Duke of Burgundy favoured Princess Isabelle's marriage in the interests of commerce, both the Dukes of Berry and Orleans opposed it.

The King of France had no need to fear for the marriage of his daughter, for Richard was for the rest of his life to treat her with a kind of flattering, romantic make-belief, having an intuitive understanding of his little Queen. They were to become very fond of one another.

Isabelle was crowned Queen of England in Westminster Abbey on January 7th 1397, but the vast expenses incurred, including the Truce, her marriage, the coronation itself, amounted to £200,000. This far exceeded the Queen's dowry. In the French archives it is related that Thomas Merke, now Bishop of Carlisle, was appointed King's Proctor to request and receive on November 17th, 100,000 gold francs owed by Charles VI as part of the agreed dowry. It is interesting to note that Shakespeare, taking legitimate dramatic licence, makes her a mature woman in *The Tragedy of Richard II*, instead of a mere child.

IX   Richard's Revenge

The King was absolutely consistent in one thing - his slow calculated revenge against the ruthless enemies who had deprived him of his dearest friends during the Merciless Parliament. Indeed, he remained as loyal to their memory in death as he had been true to them in life. He never forgot the hounding to death of his old tutor Simon Burley and he persuaded the monks of the Abbey of St. Mary Graces, by the Tower of London where he was buried, to celebrate the anniversary of his death and to inscribe his name in their martyrology.

Anthony Steel wrote a scholarly biography of *Richard II*, particularly regarding his political function, but the hypothesis he puts forward that he suffered from the growth of a neurosis "checked at first by the support and sympathy of his first wife Anne" but which developed more rapidly after her death is only partly correct.[1] Certainly his character deteriorated after 1394. In Steel's opinion, Richard's schizoid mind suffered during periods of mental stress "from a feeling that the outer world had less and less reality". He was certainly highly emotional and deeply sensitive, but to regard him later as "a mumbling neurotic sinking rapidly into a state of acute melancholia" must surely be exaggerated. It is not possible to excuse Richard's violent temper, but John Harvey opined that the frequent outbursts are consistent with the excruciating pain of calculus in the kidney. After Queen Anne's death his health almost certainly deteriorated because for the period 1395-96 the accounts of his wardrobe reveal enormous fees paid to his chief physician John Middelton, Geoffrey Melton, his second physician, his surgeon William Bridewardyn and others.

To understand Richard, it is best to remember the many different hereditary strains in his blood. Through his mother and father there were both English and French strains, and through his mother's grandfather John Wake of Liddell he had Welsh blood, being descended from the Celtic princes and Llewellyn the Great.[2]

It is perhaps due to these hereditary factors that the King found it easier to understand the Celtic mind.

Certainly Richard's appointments showed no indication of neurosis during 1395-97. Most of his ministers were very able, particularly Edmund de Stafford now Chancellor, while Guy Mone, later Bishop of St. David's held the office of Keeper of the Privy Seal. Another of Richard's friends, William Scrope of Bolton, served him as Vice-Chamberlain and Baldwin Raddington, Burley's nephew, was close to Richard, as Keeper of the Wardrobe. Roger Walden, a later Archbishop of Canterbury, served the King as Secretary. Richard's position was strong in 1397, for he had the active support of at least five of his bishops. The King, moreover, was much attached to John de Waltham, Bishop of Salisbury, a former Master of the Rolls and Lord Treasurer, but he was much criticized for ordering that he should be buried in Westminster Abbey. Jealousy was the motive because John de Waltham was the first person not of royal blood to be buried in a royal chapel[3] (St. Edward).

One appointment may have given Richard anxiety: when Archbishop Arundel was elected Archbishop of Canterbury by the Chapter at Canterbury. One of Richard's most loyal friends, John de Montague, Third Earl of Salisbury, sharing his master's ardent resolve to make peace with France, took a hand in the royal marriage to Isabelle. Salisbury, a Lollard supporter, kept a Lollard priest in his household. Extremely cultured, he composed his 'rondeau' in French. Whilst in France, he became the patron of the French poet and writer Christine de Pisan, later taking her son into his household to be educated.

Adam of Usk criticizes Richard very harshly for keeping a private army in the form of the Cheshire archers and Welsh pikemen, though Adam is silent about the private armies maintained by his barons. The King's 'Cheshire archers' acted as a royal bodyguard. Many of them were the sons of expert archers who had fought at Crécy for the Black Prince. They were devoted to the King, calling him by the familiar name of 'Dycun'.

According to Adam,[4]

the King meanwhile, ever hastening to his fall, among other burdens that he heaped upon his kingdom, kept in his following four hundred unruly men of the County of Cheshire, very evil, and in all places, they oppressed his subjects unpunished, and beat and robbed them. These men, whithersoever the King went night and day, as if at war, kept watch to arms around him, everywhere committing adulteries, murders and other evils without end . . .

Richard probably regarded it as gross interference if anybody was bold enough to nourish animosity against them, treating it as a personal affront. Adam of Usk considered it the chief cause of his ruin. The hostile Walsingham alleges that, in 1397, the Parliament House was surrounded by these men of Chester, forming the King's bodyguard.

Richard bided his time, knowing instinctively when to strike at his enemies, when the hour was ripe. Parliament assembled in January for the first time in two years. The Speaker was Sir John Bushy, a knight of the Shire and several times Sheriff of Lincoln. He had represented Lincolnshire in every Parliament except the Merciless Parliament[5] when he supported the 'appellants'. He was now the King's man, an experienced Speaker, having served before in this capacity, immensely hardworking and possessing the ability to manage the Commons. Richard found him a useful servant and secured his appointment. To the Lancastrian Chroniclers, he was a mere creature of the King, servile and avaricious. Shakespeare in *The Tragedy of Richard II* makes him his mouthpiece. Holinshed wrote of Bushy:

> When he proposed any matter unto the King, did not attribute to him Titles of honour due and accustomed, but invented unused terms and such strange names as were rather agreable to the divine majesty of God than to any earthly potentate.

It was on February 1st that a royal clerk, Thomas Haxey, not a member of the Commons, brought a petition containing several complaints. He alleged that sheriffs and escheators were continuing in office for more than a year, when an Act during Edward III's reign had ruled they were to hold office for a year only. Richard argued quite reasonably that continuity and experience were neces-

118

sary in local government. Haxey said that too many bishops and ladies were maintained in the royal household, and mounted a strong attack on the extravagance of Richard's Court. This infuriated Richard, causing him to fly into one of his characteristic rages. He demanded the name of the author of the petition. Unfortunately, the King never learnt to control his temper, and there was no Anne now to mitigate his anger. If Peter de la Mare, the bold Speaker during the last years of Richard's grandfather, had been alive, he would have championed the privileges of the Commons and refused to divulge Haxey's name. However, Speaker Bushy was a paid Knight of the royal household and apologized too fulsomely on behalf of Parliament.

It was rash and unwise of Richard to persuade his Council to ordain that anybody responsible for inciting the Commons to attack the royal prerogative was guilty of treason. Haxey was tried in the White Chamber at Westminster before the King, the Lords Temporal and the Commons, and condemned to death. Richard's anger, like lightning in a freak storm, had soon spent itself. Archbishop Arundel intervened to claim him as a clergyman and he was pardoned at the end of May. It seems probable that some sinister and influential person, such as the Duke of Gloucester or the ambivalent, double-dealing Earl of Nottingham instigated Haxey to make these injudicious attacks.

The French Chronicles, the *Chronique de la Traison et Mort de Richard II,* and Froissart reveal the mutual hatred the King and his uncle Gloucester had for one another. The author of *La Traison* is unknown, but he was probably a native of France and a Benedictine, for he later shows a kindred sympathy for Richard's friend the Benedictine Thomas Merke, Bishop of Carlisle. This source, so invaluable to a biographer, is sometimes biased, but it is an important eye witness account of the last three years of Richard II's reign. Perhaps the author came over to England in 1396 with little Queen Isabelle.

It was unwise of Gloucester to exasperate the King at a royal banquet held in Westminster in June, for he tactlessly criticized Richard's foreign policy. During April 1397 he had surrendered the fortress of Brest to the Duke of Brittany. Brest and Cherbourg had been pledged to England for the duration of the war on condi-

119

tion that a loan of about £20,000 and lands in Norfolk and elsewhere should be granted to the Duke. Now that the loan had been redeemed, there existed no justification for retaining Brest, especially with the signing of the new twenty-eight truce with France.

There were present at the banquet many soldiers, who had held Brest for the King. According to *La Traison*, Gloucester pointed out these soldiers whereupon Richard said: "Good uncle (*Bel Oncle*) what companions do you mean?" Gloucester complained that the men had been badly paid, whereupon Richard replied, reasonably enough, that they would be paid in full. Meanwhile, four good villages near London would be given up to them where they could live at the King's expense. Gloucester's words have been preserved: "Sire, you ought first to hazard your life in capturing a city from your enemies, by feat of arms or by force, before you think of surrendering or selling any city which your ancestors, the Kings of England, have gained or conquered."[6] Gloucester's scornful reproaches wounded Richard's pride. After asking his uncle to repeat his words, Richard retorted, irately: "Do you think that I am a merchant or a traitor that I wish to sell my land? By St. John the Baptist, no, no, since the Duke of Brittany had fully redeemed his pledge it was but just that the city of Brest should be restored to him." Though they parted fairly amicably, the bitterness and rancour remained. Gloucester was a marked man.

He now retired to his estate in Pleshy, Essex, where he continued to conspire against the King. Gloucester was on friendly terms with his godfather John de la Moote, Abbot of St. Albans, and it so happened that Brother John Wortng, Prior of the Abbey of Westminster, was a great friend of both Gloucester and the Abbot of St. Albans. Falling down on his knees before the Duke after dinner, the Prior fearfully revealed that he had experienced a strange vision, "that the kingdom would be lost by Our Lord the King Richard". If this account in *La Traison* can be trusted, it at least reveals how unpopular Richard's policies were in the country. Gloucester had certainly done his utmost to undermine his nephew in London. The Abbots of St. Albans, too, had always resented Richard's obvious preference for Westminster. Walsingham mentions one earlier incident, in 1383, when Richard, one night, had borrowed a palfrey from an abbot of St. Albans and never returned it. Perhaps mindful of his debt, Richard had, however, presented six years later a tun of Gascon wine to Robert Dyngle, then Abbot.

La Traison tells of a conspiracy hatched in Arundel Castle during August 1397 when Gloucester, Henry Bolingbroke, the Earls of Arundel and Nottingham, Archbishop Arundel and the two churchmen were all present. Steel treats the affair with great caution, though he does not reject the story.[7] After Mass, the conspirators[8] retired to a Council chamber and there plotted "to seize the noble King Richard" and the Dukes of Lancaster and York, intending to consign them to perpetual imprisonment. The lords of the Council were to be executed. It seems that if these facts were the truth, the conspirators comprising the former Lords Appellant of 1388, fearing Richard's vengeance, had decided to act first.

It was typical of Mowbray, Earl of Nottingham, Arundel's son-in-law, to divulge the whole affair to Richard as he was dining with his half-brother, the Earl of Huntingdon, in his magnificent house known as Cold Harborough[9] in the parish of All-Hallows. According to *La Traison* the King said to Nottingham: "Take care what you say, for if I find it true, I will pardon you; but if I find it otherwise, assuredly you shall repent it." It was the moment to strike. After consulting with his Council, Richard immediately ordered the arrest of the Earls of Arundel and Warwick. Richard himself, attended by a large number of men-at-arms and archers, rode rapidly to Pleshy Castle, intending to surprise Gloucester. The Chroniclers offer varying accounts. Froissart relates that Richard first went to a manor in Essex named Havering-atte-bower on the pretext of hunting deer, and arrived one hot afternoon at Pleshy where he had the unsuspecting nobleman arrested while riding to London. The account in *La Traison* says that the King rode into the courtyard of Pleshy while trumpets sounded their fanfare. He was attended by a company of men-at-arms and many archers. Gloucester hastily rose from his bed, and bending his knee before the King as he sallied forth "in his linen clothes" and a mantle thrown over his shoulders, greeted him with deference. He was followed by his Duchess with her ladies. Telling him to put on his clothes, Richard requested his uncle to accompany him. On the way to London, there was no further need to disguise his intent-

121

ions. Gloucester was arrested and handed over to the Earl of Nottingham, to be immediately taken in his custody to Calais where he was captain. The *La Traison* account, however, says that the King's uncle was first taken to the Tower by the Earl Marshal Nottingham.

According to the Rolls of Parliament, if they have not been tampered with, Richard told the Archbishop of Canterbury to bring his brother, Richard Earl of Arundel, to a private conference, swearing by oath that no harm should be done to his person or his property. He was immediately arrested. Archbishop Arundel later accused the King of reckless breach of faith, according to one Chronicle.[10] It is true that a formal pardon had been granted the Earl in 1394, but he had so often offended the King and conspired against him that we can have little sympathy for him.

The last Parliament of Richard's reign assembled at Westminster on September 17th 1397. The pressing business was the appointment of eight new Lords Appellant, all partisans of the King. They were Rutland, Kent, Salisbury, Huntingdon, Nottingham, Somerset, together with Sir Thomas Despenser and Lord William Scrope. Their purpose was to appeal Gloucester, Arundel and Warwick of treason. How interesting it is that exactly the same procedure was followed as during the Merciless Parliament nine years before. The King was aware, however, that Gloucester was already dead, having been almost certainly murdered at Calais.

The noblemen were accused on four grounds: of compassing and designing to slay the King, to depose him, to withdraw homage, and to ride against him.[11] The evidence offered, however, related to the events of 1386-88, rather than the more circumstantial evidence of the Arundel Castle conspiracy.

On Friday September 21st 1397, there strode into Parliament the four new Appellants dressed in red robes of silk, banded with white silk and powdered with letters of gold.

John of Gaunt, Duke of Lancaster, as High Steward presided at the trial of his enemy Richard Fitzalan, Earl of Arundel, firstly ordering him to be deprived of his Knight's belt and his scarlet hood. Arundel with all his faults was no coward. The people loved him for his bravery in naval warfare. As Brembre had done in 1388 so did Arundel now demand trial by battle, but it was refused him.

Then the defendant and John of Gaunt hurled insults at one another, Arundel stubbornly maintaining that he had been freely
granted a pardon in 1394. He was no traitor. If treasons were in
question, Gaunt needed pardon more than he did. Sir John Bushy
in the course of the trial reminded Arundel that "his pardon had
been remitted by the King, the Lords, and us his faithful Commons". "Where be those faithful Commons?" retorted the furious
nobleman. "They, I know, art sore grieved for me, and I know that
thou hast ever been false."

The Earl of Derby's attack on his old colleague was deplorable,
for he had joined the Lords Appellant in 1387, being present in
the Tower during Richard's ultimate humiliation. Evidently he
thought his best course was to turn King's evidence. No doubt he
resented Arundel calling his father a traitor on numerous occasions.
According to Adam of Usk, Derby accused Arundel of saying at
Huntingdon, "Where first we were gathered to revolt, that it would
be better first to seize the King." Arundel answered: "Thou, Earl
of Derby, thou liest at thy peril! Never had I a thought, concerning our lord the King, save what was to his welfare and honour."

It was a foregone conclusion that Arundel would be condemned to death. He was hurried off to execution on Tower Hill,
after being blindfolded by his son-in-law, the Earl of Nottingham.
Froissart is mistaken when he mentions he was beheaded in Cheapside. The Monk of Kirkstall Abbey wrote with satisfaction that the
nobleman was buried in exactly the same spot as Simon Burley.

This Chronicler also relates that it was alleged against Archbishop Arundel that when appointed principal Councillor to the
King he had betrayed Richard's confidences to his brother.[12]
Though he had loyally attempted to save the Earl, his first loyalty
was surely to the King. However, he was impeached, not appealed,
like the others of treason. The King has been criticized for prevent-
ing Thomas Arundel from defending himself, but it is difficult to
justify his conduct in 1386-88 when the Lords Appellant had the
King in their power. If the account in *La Traison* is true, the Archbishop was present in Arundel Castle when his brother and others
were conspiring against Richard. He was sentenced to forfeiture
and exile overseas, and Roger Walden succeeded him as Archbishop
of Canterbury. If Thomas Arundel disliked Richard in 1397, he

now became a dangerous enemy intriguing against him abroad. His biographer* wrote "that his treatment shows the royal case at its worst". I wonder! She says, "The earl was granted a cursory trial, and at least some opportunity to reply. The fact that he (the Archbishop) was twice prevented from defending himself suggests the uncertainty which hung about his case." Bushy may have feared that Arundel's subtle mind and cunning would prevail upon the Court, and he would come to no harm.

The Earl of Warwick, now an old man, appeared utterly craven at his trial. Adam of Usk, an eye witness, says that he confessed everything . . . "wailing and weeping and whining". The King had no difficulty in extracting a confession from him, that it was the Duke of Gloucester, the prior of Westminster, and the Abbot of St. Albans who had tempted him to treason. This seems to confirm *La Traison* and the plotting at St. Albans. Richard could not conceal his delight at the confession of the unhappy man, exclaiming - "By St. John the Baptist, Thomas of Warwick, Your Confession is more pleasing to me than the value of all the lands of the duke of Gloucester and the earl of Arundel."[13] Anthony Steel opines that a more detailed admission of recent treachery, whether plotted at St. Albans or elsewhere, was made by Warwick, ignored by the Lancastrian Chroniclers and subsequently expunged from the Parliamentary Rolls.

Warwick's admissions were useful enough to preserve his life. He was sentenced to exile in the Isle of Man, not the Isle of Wight as Froissart wrote. According to Froissart, the Earl of Salisbury, high in the King's favour, interceded with Richard for Warwick's life. He was soon transferred to the Tower and later freed by Henry IV. The Kirkstall monk says that a fixed annuity was promised Warwick, though probably never paid. He praises Richard in this instance for "mixing the oil of mercy with the wine of Justice".[14] Little Queen Isabelle even had a hand in praying her husband to save Warwick's life, showing her influence at a tender age.

Why should Richard have qualms of conscience about Arundel? Walsingham mentions that the King's sleep was disturbed by visions of the dead earl. He had no need to reproach himself. Yet to allay his fears, he ordered Northumberland to go to the Church of the Augustine Friars in Moorgate where Arundel's body lay

* Miss M.E. Aston, *Thomas Arundel*, (Oxford, 1967)

buried. Rumours abounded that his severed head had been joined to his body, for superstitious people believed that it was divine reprobation for an unjust act. Richard's vengeance, however, had been far less harsh than the cruel executions during the Merciless Parliament.

If Gloucester had been compelled to face a trial in England, it would have been embarrassing for Richard, not least for his brothers York and Lancaster. According to Froissart, Gloucester, in the custody of Nottingham, the Earl Marshal in Calais Castle, was about to wash his hands before dinner when four men rushed out from a room and, twisting a towel round his neck, pulled so hard that he staggered to the floor. Thereafter strangling him, they laid him on a feathered bed. His death is actually a mystery, but he was probably murdered. It is more difficult to identify the actual instigator of the crime. The most obvious candidate was the Earl of Nottingham, and both *Adam of Usk* and *The Annales of Ricardi II and Henrici IV* accuse him. Again, Richard's favourite the Earl of Rutland certainly had a motive, for he was appointed to Gloucester's high office of Constable of England almost immediately after the arrest of the King's uncle.[15] However, there is little evidence to connect him with the crime.

It is of course possible that Gloucester died a natural death, for he was ill at Pleshy when requested to accompany Richard to London. If suffocated or strangled, Richard must bear the ultimate responsibility, though his uncle richly deserved his fate, having been his nephew's most vindictive enemy. The actual agent may have been William Serle, later executed by Henry IV for treason. A more likely candidate than a man named Halle, who is reputed to have made a confession.[16] *La Traison* merely says that the King sent his uncle to Calais, and there caused him to be put to death.

The actual date is uncertain, but Richard sent a Kentish Justice of the Peace, Sir William Rickhill, to Calais to obtain his uncle's confession.[17] The Justice received a writ at Essingham in Kent (August 17th 1395) from Richard for that purpose. All sorts of rumours abounded that he was already dead. As was later revealed in Parliament, Rickhill obtained a confession from Gloucester in which he fully admitted his guilt and treason. As Lingard wrote,

Gloucester could plead eloquently enough on his own behalf to his nephew for mercy where he had shown none to others.[18] The most likely date of Gloucester's death is September 17th (the Feast of St. Lambert) or immediately afterwards. The accusation that the King falsified the date of his uncle's murder in order to pretend that a crime had not been perpetrated does not ring true.

Richard now created five new dukes: his half-brother Sir John Holland (Huntingdon) became Duke of Exeter, the Earl of Kent (Richard's nephew) became Duke of Surrey, the Earl of Derby received the dukedom of Hereford, the turncoat Thomas Mowbray (Nottingham) was created Duke of Norfolk, while the King's much loved Rutland became Duke of Albemarle (Shakespeare called him 'Aumerle'). These honours were intended as rewards for those who had supported him.

His decision to legitimize the sons of John of Gaunt by his former mistress, Katherine Swynford, now his wife, was by no means relished by his cousin Henry. Gaunt's eldest illegitimate son, the Earl of Somerset, now became the Marquis of Dorset. Others rewarded included Sir Thomas Percy, now Earl of Worcester, and Thomas Despenser who was given the earldom of Gloucester. To reward himself, Richard annexed the vast estates of the Earl of Arundel, joining them to the royal principality of Cheshire. Arundel's estates on the Marches of Shropshire and in the Northern Marches of Wales were for ever incorporated in the new principality.

By raising the county palatine to a higher status (September 25th 1397), the King evidently showed a desire to honour the men of Chester. It also revealed his great affection for the county and the men of Chester were to be staunchly loyal to their King.

By the autumn, the King had reached the zenith of his power and influence. The King's love of dramatic gesture never waned. *La Traison* relates how the King held a magnificent review of the Londoners. In the evening there was a great banquet at Court when the heralds received lavish gifts from the lords and ladies, and cried 'largesse', and my lady of Exeter received the prize as the best dancer and the best singer.[19]

X   His Downfall

Richard II was intensely ambitious. As a boy King, married to Anne, his first wife, the daughter of the Holy Roman Emperor Charles IV, King of Bohemia, he may have already nourished thoughts that he, too, might soar one day to such a lofty dignity. Now in 1397, aged thirty, he claimed to be "entier emperour de son roiaulme."[1] This was a serious project. For three years from 1394 to 1397 Richard began intimate relations with Cologne, entrusting Nottingham and Rutland with the negotiations in the Rhineland.[2] Nothing came of the grand project.

One English Chronicler, the Rev. John Silvester Davies, writing before 1471, implies that Richard lived in a dream world of his own

> in Solemn daies and grete festis, in the which he 'wered his crowne, and wente in his rial aray . . . and make in his chambir, a trone wherynne he was wont to sitte fro aftir mete unto evensong spekynge to no man, but overloking alle men, and yf he loked on eny man, what astat or degre that evir he were of, he most knele.

No other Chronicler mentions this.

The *Kirkstall Chronicle* written by a Cistercian monk in Yorkshire has an extremely interesting account of the final years of Richard's reign by a man whose sympathies up to 1397 were with the King, even with Richard's craving for absolute power.

> Of late the sun had been concealed by a cloud, that is to say the king's majesty beneath an alien power, but now in arms he bounds on the mountains (*armis saliens in montibus*) and leaps over the hills (*et transiliens colles*) and tossing the clouds on his horns he shows more brightly the light of the sun.[3]

When claiming to exercise absolute power, Richard was to make a series of mistakes and misjudgements that were eventually to lead to his ruin and undoing. No King, even a Plantagenet, can claim with impunity that the laws of his country reside only in his own breast. Did Richard ever in fact say this? We have only the 'gravamina', the accusations during the deposition and proceedings. His actions, however, too often show no respect for the laws of England even in the early days.

The Monk of Westminster, sometimes lavish in Richard's praise, relates one incident in 1384 when twenty-five prisoners, including five priests, were brought out of Newgate and beheaded at Foul Oak in Kent, accused by one of the King's yeomen of having robbed him with violence. Surely the young King should have insisted on a trial.

During the session of Parliament at Shrewsbury, the King's financial problems were at least eased. He was granted the duties on wool, woodfells and leather *for life*.[4] It was a useful addition to the Royal Exchequer. Richard's obsession with pardons was ill-advised. During this Parliament the judgements made during the Merciless Parliament were repealed and offenders, for the most part, pardoned. However, the King was mistaken in insisting on the pardons being purchased and fifty unnamed, nervous persons did not share this clemency, causing tension and resentment. Everybody had to swear an oath of loyalty to the King on the Cross of Canterbury where during the Westminster Parliamentary Sessions (September 1397) a similar oath had been sworn on the shrine of St. Edward. It is curious that Roger Mortimer, Earl of March, Richard's heir presumptive and the King's Lieutenant in Ireland, was specially summoned to Shrewsbury to take the oath. Adam of Usk,[5] whose first patron was the Third Earl of March, thinks that Mortimer was involved in the St. Albans plot, but this is unlikely. The new Earl of Worcester (Sir Thomas Percy), having been appointed by proxy by the clergy, administered the oaths.

There occurred just before Christmas (1397) a dramatic event, fated to have terrible consequences. Shakespeare with the infallible instincts of a great dramatist begins his *Tragedy of Richard II* with it. It so happened that the new Dukes of Hereford and Norfolk met by chance travelling by horseback between Brentford and

128

London. They were two original Lords Appellant, the only ones who had survived Richard's vengeance so far. Although the King now found Norfolk a useful instrument, he had never really forgiven him for siding with his opponents in 1387-88. Hereford, more intelligent and wary than his fellow duke, kept his thoughts to himself, confiding in a few people. So it was recklessly indiscreet of Mowbray to blab fearfully to Bolingbroke, according to the latter's account:

> "We are on the point of being undone."
>
> "Why so," replied the startled Hereford.
>
> "On account of the affair of Radcot Bridge," said Norfolk.
>
> "How can that be," answered Hereford, "since he has granted us pardon and has declared in Parliament that we behaved as good and loyal subjects."

Norfolk told him that, despite this pardon, their fate would be similar to the others. He unwisely added that the King's younger friends were daily urging him to secure his position by taking action against Hereford and himself. He talked darkly about a plot to kill both Hereford and his father, the Duke of Lancaster. The two lords spoke in hushed voices, fearful lest they might be overheard. Theirs was a treacherous world.

If Norfolk erred in confiding in Hereford, the latter behaved dishonourably in relating his version of the story to the King, for he was breaking the knightly code. Both noblemen now accused each other of treason.

It is unsatisfactory that the only source is Hereford's. Kenneth McFarlane in his *Kings and Lollard Knights* is very loath to accept his account of what transpired as the truth, conceiving it "so disingenuous as to raise the question of his veracity" (see pp. 43 et seq.). To accept Hereford's account is to suppose him extraordinarily gullible. He even implies that it was Hereford not Norfolk who started the conversation on the way to London. Froissart*, too, supports this version, saying that Hereford told Norfolk of his suspicions and it was Norfolk who was incredulous.

* See the account of Lord Berners in *Chronicle of Froissart*, Vol. II, p. 711.

The whole affair is fully described in *The Chronique de la Traison*.[6] There is no reason to doubt that Richard tried to reconcile his cousin and Norfolk on several occasions. Froissart, however, criticizes Richard for not first of all attempting to appease these two lords without taking into account their deep enmity. The King commanded Henry to put his accusations in writing, to be adjudicated upon at the Parliament adjourned to Shrewsbury. Both noblemen were arrested, but Hereford found bail in his father, his uncle York, his cousin Albemarle and the Duke of Surrey, while Norfolk was not so fortunate, being imprisoned in Windsor Castle. Consequently, Hereford was free to attend the Shrewsbury Parliament, but Norfolk could not do so.

They both appeared before the King at a High Court of Chivalry at Windsor in late April 1398 when Sir John Bushy, Speaker of the Commons, played a prominent part in the proceedings. Hereford now made two more extremely serious accusations against Norfolk: first, that he had been responsible for the death of "my dear and beloved uncle the duke of Gloucester", and secondly, that Mowbray had embezzled public funds entrusted to him as Captain of Calais for paying the garrison. The Chroniclers differ as to how much money he was accused of taking. Fabyan mentions four thousand marks a year, since Mowbray had been captain of Calais for twenty years. The eight hundred thousand nobles mentioned in *La Traison* is almost certainly exaggerated. The King now losing his patience, having for the last time tried to reconcile them, said, "By Saint John the Baptist I will try no more." The quarrel was referred to a committee, who decided that Hereford had not proved his accusations. Both Hereford and Norfolk wanted trial by battle. On his part Hereford was willing to prove the truth of his accusations "by his body" between any sunrise and sunset (*"entre deux soleils"*). Norfolk in rebutting Hereford's accusations claimed that the people of Calais had never lodged any complaints against him. However, the charge was later proved against him. In an attempt to justify his actions, Norfolk claimed that during his mission to France for Richard's marriage to the Princess Isabelle and his negotiations in Germany, he had never received either silver or gold from the King. He did admit that he had once laid an ambush to slay the Duke of Lancaster, but he had forgiven him. The Kirkstall Chronicler describes Norfolk as *horrificus* (frightful), possibly fearing to offend the Lancastrians.

Richard feared his cousin Henry. He had lately been warned by a Court astrologer to beware of toads, for a toad would destroy him.[7] When Henry had attended a Christmas banquet wearing a gown 'broderyd (embroidered) al abowte with toadys',[8] the King remembered the astrologer's warning. So, he favoured Mowbray on whom he had once lavished splendid presents, but it was stressed to Richard by his advisers that he must show an air of complete impartiality. They knew that Henry was very popular in the country, much beloved by the Londoners.

This fight to the death between Norfolk and Hereford attracted enormous interest in England and throughout Europe. Both noblemen excelled in jousts and were famed for their prowess in arms. The trial by battle was to take place in Gosforth Field, outside the Warwickshire town of Coventry. It was a resplendent scene on Sunday September 15th, the evening before the combat. Richard was staying the night with his close friend Sir William Bagot at the Castle of Baginton just outside the walls of Coventry when the two protagonists rode out to take their official leave. Norfolk then visited the Carthusian monastery of St. Anne's where he heard three masses before going to his tent to don his armour with the help of his esquire Jacques Felm of Bohemia.[9]

Froissart relates that both dukes were splendidly armed, no doubt vying to outshine one another. Hereford's friend, Galeazzo Visconti, Duke of Milan, had supplied him with his coat and mail, even sending him the Chevalier François and four of the best armourers in Lombardy, while Norfolk had the most skilful armourers from Germany.

The Constable, the Duke of Albemarle, and the new Marshal, the Duke of Surrey, wore liveries of short robes, richly decorated with the Garter while their twenty followers "were dressed in silk and Kendal cloth, embroidered with silver".

The pageantry on this dramatic September day appealed enormously to Richard. Amidst much pomp the King, attended by Roger Walden, the new Archbishop of Canterbury, by a French nobleman, the Count of St. Pol and by all his nobles, sat majestically on his throne on a great dais. Surrounding Richard were twenty thousand archers and many men-at-arms.

It is difficult to analyse the King's sentiments, but they would have been mixed. A natural dread lest his cousin Bolingbroke should triumph in the fight, to be acclaimed by the people, might have seemed to him the most probable outcome, for Henry was the more experienced jouster. But if by any chance Mowbray was the victor and Henry killed, it would be a rude shock for his father John of Gaunt. Could Richard then continue to depend on his uncle's full support? For some time he had been pondering that it best served him to get rid of both Hereford and Norfolk.

Now among those close to the King on that day was a special French envoy, Sir Nicholas Payzel, charged by Richard's father-in-law, Charles VI, to persuade him to prevent the trial by battle taking place. Perhaps Charles considered that the risks were too great, especially owing to their high birth and their proximity to the thrones of England and France. Similar advice may well have been urged by several of Richard's counsellors.

The trumpets sounded. The author of *La Traison*, almost certainly an eye witness, relates that the herald cried by order of the King, the Earl Marshal and the Constable that the tents should be taken away, a signal that the adversaries should "let go their chargers and that each should perform their duty". Placing his lance upon his thigh, pushing forward his shield, and making the sign of the cross, Hereford advanced seven or eight paces towards his adversary. One can see them so vividly with Shakespeare, "their beavers down, their eyes of fire sparkling through sights of steel".[10] Then, to the fury of the thousands of spectators, deprived of their blood lust, the King, whose sense of the theatre was never more marked, rose up, crying "Ho! Ho!" and cast down his staff, a signal that the battle must stop. Both combatants were conducted to their seats, while the King decided what sentences to impose on the two noblemen. After almost two hours of suspense, Sir John Bushy came forward holding a large roll of parchment "a full fathom long". After praising Mowbray and Bolingbroke for their valiant behaviour and willingness to do their duty like brave knights, he turned to the sentences.

It was decreed by the King and Council that Hereford should be banished for ten years from the realm "and if he return to the country before the ten years are passed, he shall be hung and beheaded". No doubt there was a loud clamour and many protests, but Henry was far from guiltless. Why had he been present with Gloucester, Arundel and the other conspirators in Arundel Castle in 1397? A much harsher sentence was imposed on Norfolk, that of banishment for life. Rather surprising, perhaps, since Richard had been once so attached to him, even if he was more culpable. He was given the option of living in Prussia, in Bohemia, in Hungary or "travelling to the land of the Saracens or unbelievers". All Norfolk's lands were forfeited to the King, but he was allowed £1,000 per annum for his own use. He was a broken man. After taking final leave of the King at Windsor, he sailed from the Suffolk coast to Holland, and from there made a pilgrimage to Jerusalem. After a year of exile he died in Venice. On the same day the lords took leave of the King, Petrus de Bosco, Bishop of Dax, the Pope's legate, presented to the little Queen Isabelle, at Windsor, a parrot then considered owing to its extreme rarity, a present suitable for such a great lady.

For John of Gaunt the banishment of his eldest son was a bitter blow, but there are no indications that he disagreed with the sentence or protested at it. When his uncle interceded for Henry, the King showed no hardness of spirit, graciously remitting four years of the sentence. Nor did he treat Hereford ungenerously, allowing him £2,000 per annum. It is recorded that the King paid him a thousand marks on November 14th 1398 and £1,586 13s. 4d. seven months later.[11] Later, Richard regretted that he had promised his cousin that he would enjoy his father's great landed estates if he were to inherit them abroad whilst in exile.[12] In medieval times, Gaunt was quite an old man. If his father were to die, Henry would obtain vast Palatinate powers. To give Hereford and Norfolk the power of attorney to receive any inheritances that might fall to them in exile was very difficult to revoke.

Bolingbroke was given a sorrowful farewell at Dover by more than 40,000 people, according to Froissart. Embarking for Calais, Paris and the royal Court of France, the people lamented: "Gentle earl, why shall we leave you? Ye never dyd nor thought yvell."

Among those taking disconsolate leave of Hereford were the Earl of Northumberland and his son Harry Percy. Northumberland was very friendly with John of Gaunt's son, signing his letters "Vostre Mathathias", referring to some ancient prophecy according to the Catholic historian Lingarn. Hotspur was much the same age as Bolingbroke, but no intimacy existed between them. Married as he was to the Lady Elizabeth Mortimer, descended from Lionel of Clarence, Hotspur probably mistrusted him. Did Bolingbroke try to flatter Percy? Shakespeare puts into the mouth of the warrior:

> Why, what a candy deal of courtesy
> This fawning greyhound then did proffer me,
> Look, 'when his infant fortune came to age'
> and 'Gentle Harry Percy' and 'Kind cousin'
> O! the devil take such cozeners.[13]

With the banishment of the last of the Lords Appellant, Richard seemed triumphant, but there were treacherous shoals ahead beckoning him to his destruction.

It is interesting to analyse the reasons for Richard's downfall. In hindsight, one can see it was folly on his part, from 1398 onwards, not to cultivate friendly relations with the citizens of London. For instance, his removal of the Westminster Parliament to Shrewsbury was keenly resented. By 1398 the King was hated by the people of London. Though by nature extremely generous and his hospitality princely, he was more and more criticized for the extravagance of his Court. Holinshed relates:

> in his kitchen there were three hundred servitors . . . of ladies, chamberers and launderers, there were about one hundred at the least. Yeomen and groomes were clothed in silkes, with clothe of grain and skarlet, oversumptuous, ye may be sure for their estates.[14]

A recent discovery of a fourteenth century parchment roll in Westbury near Buckingham, now in the Public Record Office, provides a full account of Richard's spending for over fifteen months. (See *Daily Telegraph*, April 21st 1988. Also PRC/30/26/236.) The roll is in Latin and provides further corroboration of the King's generosity to those he liked. Some would call it extravagance. On one occasion he gave William of Wykeham, founder of Winchester College, a £100 set of vestments and altar cloths inlaid with gold, while the Prior of the Abbey of Leeds in Kent was presented with an elegant cape decorated with green dragons.

Dr. Lingarn, no favourable critic, wrote of Richard,

It would however, be difficult to prove that his expenses were greater than those of his predecessors, it is certain that his demands on the purses of his subjects were considerably less.

Contemporary princes such as the Duke of Orleans, maintained magnificent households of two hundred and forty servants (including three jesters). Even when he went on crusade in Hungary he needed two hundred servants wearing his livery. His tents were of green satin, and his banners and standards embroidered with silver, gold and precious stones.

The foreign Chronicles, such as the Monk of Saint Denys (1380-1422), allude to the evil disposition of the Londoners towards Richard, but people in the north of England later complained that Henry IV had only been elected by the villeins of the City of London. For Richard, it was a misfortune that, despite his love of pageantry, he was not his subjects' idea of a popular King leading his armies to some spectacular victory. Henry Bolingbroke, as an expert jouster and with his foreign experience in warfare came much nearer to their ideal - at least in the late 1390s.

During the summer of 1397, it is recorded that Richard interfered in the election of a Mayor of London. On June 6th a very rich goldsmith, Adam Bamme, died in office, and the King chose in his stead Richard Whittington, a name familiar to every schoolboy. An ancient right of the Londoners to choose their own mayor had been established in 1215, so it was not surprising that the barons of the Exchequer refused to swear him, a duty undertaken by the King.[15] It was an excellent appointment, for Whittington was a close friend of Richard's and served him well. Perhaps he was rather subservient. When Mayor, however, he negotiated the 'loan' of ten thousand marks (£6,666 13s. 4d.) whereby the Londoners bought a full and perpetual confirmation of their liberties from the King. Where most people in the City were hostile, Dick Whittington was at least friendly.

Richard has often been condemned as a tyrant, for trampling on the liberties of his subjects, but it is surely controversial. He was desperate for money, needed by 1399 for his second expedition to Ireland, but it is not possible to justify the forced loans, amounting to £20,000, that the people had to pay from August 1397 onwards. The rich burgesses naturally resented the King's methods of raising money. He owed £6,570 of outstanding debt to the Londoners, £5,500 to seventy-one other towns and £3,180 to seventy-two individual clerks or religious houses.[16] As security, the King definitely granted letters patent under the Great Seal, so it is just possible that if the revolution had not taken place, these loans would have been repaid.[17] However, Richard's methods of raising money were entirely arbitrary, oppressive and consequently illegal. One of his most ingenious ways was the so-called detested *le pleasaunce*, the buying back of the pleasure of the King by enormous fines. This especially applied to the seventeen counties which had sided with the Lords Appellant during 1387-88.

It was deeply humiliating for the shires to be compelled to buy back their pardons by fines of £1,000 or 1,000 marks. Moreover, blank charters were inserted in these crooked pardons in which the King might write any sum of money he pleased. To explain why Richard resorted to such arbitrary means of raising money is easy enough. His expenses far exceeded the money provided for him by his Parliaments, and subsequent Kings of England, especially the Stuarts, were to suffer from similar causes. By the autumn of 1398, Richard was planning a second expedition to Ireland, and he had learnt by experience that such a campaign was extremely costly. His Treasury was only partly able to supply the funds.

It was vital for the King to go because during the summer the Irish chiefs MacMurrough and O'Neill were in open rebellion, having broken their oaths of fealty. On returning to Ireland from Shrewsbury, Richard's Lord Lieutenant, Roger Mortimer, Earl of March, was defeated and killed on July 20th, at the battle of Kel-

136

listown (or Kells). A disaster for the King because he now determined to plan a second Irish Campaign both to avenge Roger Mortimer's death and to complete the pacification so ably undertaken
in 1394. It entailed grave risks for Richard because England was in
a very unsettled state, and both he and his ministers were deeply
unpopular. Richard's policy was to make Ireland a profitable apan-
age to the English Crown. He now declared Roger's heir, Edmund
a boy of seven, his heir presumptive.

The political lampoons of the late reign of Richard II reveal
the extent of his unpopularity and that of his ministers.[18] Here is
one ON KING RICHARD'S MINISTERS, composed in June or July
1397 and published two years later.

> There is a busch that is forgrowe
> Crop hit welle, and hold hit, lowe,
> or elles hit wolle be wilde
> The long gras that is so Grene,
> Hit most be mowe, and racked clene,
> forgrowen hit hath the felld.
> The grete bagge that is so mykille
> It shall be cut and made little,
> Its bottom is almost out.

To understand this bitter satire one must understand that 'a
busch' refers to Sir John Bushy, 'the long gras that is so grene' de-
signates Sir Harry Green, also a prominent Chamber-Knight, and
'the grete bagge' is Sir William Bagot, a trusted friend of Richard's.
The heron in the poem is Henry of Lancaster, who will see that
the Bush, the Green and the bag will be suitably punished. To des-
cribe the murdered Gloucester as 'a gentle swan' is extremely iron-
ical. Other verses are interesting, one, for instance, referring to
Thomas Arundel, son of the executed earl, first imprisoned in the
safekeeping of the Duke of Exeter. He managed to escape, later
joining Hereford in his exile in France.

> The stedes colt (son of the earl) is ronnen away
> an eron (Henry of Lancaster) hath taken him to his
>   praye
> hit is a wondur 'casse'.

A poem called *Richard the Redeless* (ill-advised) is critical of royal luxury:

> For where was ever any Christian
> King that ye ever knew that held
> such an household by the half delle
> as Richard in this realm.

> Men mythen as well have hunted an hare with a
> tabre as aske any mendis (amends).

The writer of the alliterative poem on *The deposition of Richard II* is anything but respectful towards the King.

John of Gaunt, Duke of Lancaster, did not long survive his son's banishment, for his health was failing, and he died on February 2nd 1399 at Leicester Castle.[19] Gaunt's great speech reproaching his nephew Richard, in Shakespeare's deathbed scene of John of Gaunt, never actually took place. We cannot be certain what Gaunt thought of Richard's autocratic rule, for he was himself autocratic. One thing is certain, he kept his thoughts to himself. Certainly up to early 1399, Richard had not behaved unduly harshly to his cousin. Now, however, he committed an act of flagrant illegality. It is surely surprising that Richard never anticipated his elderly uncle's death, but as already mentioned he had given Hereford power of attorney during the previous autumn to receive any inheritances that might fall to him whilst exiled abroad. By his father's death at the age of fifty-nine, Hereford inherited over thirty castles and rich inheritance of Lancastrian estates, the County Palatine of Lancaster where the King's writ had no legal force. Clearly Richard visualized that Henry, when he returned from his six-year exile with unlimited powers, would be an overmighty subject and a dangerous enemy. Had Richard grown over-confident? He now acted decisively in an attempt to ruin Hereford. He firstly revived the Parliamentary Committee of 1398, created to terminate outstanding petitions and to deal with the Norfolk-Hereford dispute. His purpose was to forge the Parliament Roll, so that his cousin could no longer receive inheritances in exile. Instead of merely 'to terminate petitions' there was added 'to terminate petitions and other matters and things moved in the presence of the King in accordance with what seems best to them'. It was a form of legal chicanery for which Richard must be condemned. The Chancellor announced that the grant had been made 'inadvertently'. The "Judgement" of Coventry had in effect declared both Hereford and Norfolk traitors. A traitor could not inherit what would *ipso facto* have been forfeit to the Crown. Henry's sentence was now changed to exile for life.

The sequestration of the Lancastrian estates by the King was his crowning blunder, leading directly to his downfall. All men of property, whether great barons or men with a few acres of land, could no longer have any sense of security. It later enabled Henry, when he invaded the Kingdom, to pose as the champion of property rights. It further lent substance to those who said that Richard was reckless as to breaking his pledged word.

Far from being cold-shouldered when Henry reached Paris, he was given a splendid reception by the French. Presumably they were under the false impression that he was only temporarily under King Richard's displeasure and would speedily be recalled. Why did Richard not send a confidential message to his father-in-law Charles VI as to the true state of affairs? It seems very surprising. A French diplomat, Sir Nicholas Payzel, had been at Coventry with King Richard, and he, too, could have kept his compatriots better informed. Charles VI, who was enjoying one of his lucid periods between waves of insanity, generously put at Henry's disposal in Paris the Hotel Clisson, with an allowance of 500 francs a week. Here he lived magnificently with his two hundred retainers, dining on gold and silver plate. At Court he was an honoured guest at tournaments, hunts, minstrelsies and banquets. King Charles VI's uncle the Duke of Berry even suggested that Henry might marry his daughter.

It came as a rude shock for the French when the Earl of Salisbury, charged by King Richard to reach a settlement on Queen Isabelle's dowry, made a point of ignoring Henry, declaring before Charles VI that 'the earl of Derby (his father was still alive) was a traitor who wolde betray his natural soverayne lorde'. Henry was never to forgive Salisbury for his denunciation. Any further talk of a possible marriage with the Duke of Berry's daughter at once terminated. For a time Henry planned to leave France for Hungary to join in a campaign against the Turks, but he was deterred from pursuing this plan after he heard that his father was mortally ill. Within a month, Henry was mortified to learn that the great Lancastrian estates he had inherited from his father had been sequestrated by the King and granted to his friends.

Among those who joined Henry in Paris was the young Thomas, Earl of Arundel, but far more significant was the arrival of his uncle Thomas, the ex-Archbishop of Canterbury. This ambitious prelate could never reconcile himself to a life of obscurity or retirement abroad. Coldly resentful against King Richard for depriving him of his important post, Arundel had first visited Rome where he persuaded Pope Boniface IX to write to Richard asking him to reinstate him as Archbishop. Indignant at what he considered the Pope's interference, the King replied that Arundel was a traitor. If His Holiness wished to provide for him elsewhere, so be it. There was no place for him in England.

Travelling in great secrecy, disguised as a pilgrim monk, according to Froissart, the ex-Archbishop arrived in Paris. Outside the Hotel Clisson the sunlight glistened on the River Seine as the politically-minded Thomas Arundel plotted with Henry - now, by his father's death, Duke of Lancaster. It is evident that the ex-Archbishop had a large share in persuading Henry to invade England. He told him of the troubled state of the Kingdom, the violence and destruction occurring in many parts of the country and that justice was in abeyance through the King's fault. Froissart alleges that the Londoners, prelates and others wanted Henry to return to put a stop to this. Both Hall and Froissart state that Arundel's mission was to tempt Henry with the prospect of acquiring his cousin's crown. The nobility, prelates and magistrates, according to Hall,

> desiring him to return, and promising all their aid, power and assistance, if he, expelling King Richard as a man not meet nor convenient for such a princely office and degree, would take upon him the sceptre, rule and diadem of his native country, and first nutritive soil.

It is said that Henry, always cautious, pondered deeply as he looked out of a window overlooking gardens, then said he would consult his friends. Arundel probably wanted Henry to become King on his own terms and to regain his former position of power and influence as Archbishop of Canterbury. Henry was now secretly in touch with Richard's treacherous cousin, the Duke of Albemarle, the Earl of Northumberland and Henry's own half-brother John Beaufort, Marquis of Dorset.

At this moment so pregnant with danger, Richard would have been well advised to postpone his expedition to Ireland, even if it had been so imperative for him to go. It would have served him better to discover the effect on his cousin of the sequestration of the Lancastrian estates. Again it was folly to take such a formidable army to Ireland, and to expose his kingdom to a treacherous attack by an unscrupulous enemy. The King seems to have been singularly ill-informed about what was transpiring in France. Did Richard have no inkling of the dangers ahead? One of his worse misjudgements was to underestimate the ability of the new Duke of Lancaster. He could not conceive that without a powerful fleet to support him, his cousin would present a real challenge. He was hardly complacent, but fearful about the outcome of the Irish war; and ill at ease about his exasperated people at home. When asked one day why he was sighing, Richard replied, "Do you wonder then that I sigh, I who am fated to so many unavoidable evile?"[20]

On April 16th 1399, six weeks before he sailed for Ireland, Richard made his will, asking to be laid to rest beside his first queen, the much loved Anne of Bohemia, in Westminster Abbey.

From *The Chronique de la Traison* and other French Chronicles we see how attached Richard was to his child Queen Isabelle, and worried how she would fare while he was in Ireland. He had heard disquieting reports about Isabelle's governess the Lady Marie de Coucy, eldest daughter[21] of Enguerrand Lord of Coucy, reported to be extravagant and to be living in greater state than the Queen. So he confidentially inquired of Sir Philip de la Vache, the Queen's Chamberlain, and Master Pol, the royal physician: "Do you consider the Lady de Coucy to be sufficiently good, 'gentile' and prudent, to be guardian and governess of such a lady as

Madame, the Queen of England, my Consort?" As eldest daughter of Charles VI, Isabelle had the right from birth to the title of Madame. The general opinion was that Marie de Coucy lacked the necessary qualities, and the Lady Mortimer, widow of Roger Mortimer, Earl of March, was appointed in her place.

There is a touching account of how Richard and Isabelle walked hand in hand from Windsor Castle to the Lower Court, and thence to the Deanery of St. George. The King took the Queen in his arms and kissed her more than forty times, saying sadly, "Adieu, Madame, until we meet again: I commend me to you." The Queen began to weep, saying: "Alas! my lord, will you leave me here?" Richard answered: "By no means, Madame, but I will go first, and you, Madame, shall come there afterwards." The writer of the Chronicle, obviously an eye witness, says: "I never saw so great a lord make so much of, nor show such great affection to a lady, as did King Richard to his Queen." Tragically, it was to be the last time Richard was ever to see his little bride.

XI   Betrayal

It was deeply unfortunate for Richard that there was nobody suitable to appoint as head of State during his absence in Ireland except his last surviving uncle, Edward Langley, Duke of York. Although York had acted as Regent during his nephew's first expedition to Ireland in 1394, he was a weak, ineffectual man, though always well-meaning. However, administrative affairs were in the hands of the efficient Sir John Bushy, Sir Henry Green, and Sir William Bagot, and Richard's Chancellor Edmund de Stafford, Bishop of Exeter was extremely able.

It was unfortunate, too, that the royal army led by the King included most of his close friends such as his nephew the Duke of Surrey, now Richard's Lieutenant and Justice in Ireland, his half-brother the Duke of Exeter, the Earls of Salisbury, Gloucester and Worcester, the only member of the powerful Percy family to accompany his master to Ireland. Richard's treacherous cousin Edward Duke of Albemarle was there, already plotting to abandon the King. The field was open for an unscrupulous adventurer to invade the Kingdom. Richard could not have left England at a worst juncture.

The Earl of Northumberland and his son 'Hotspur' remonstrated so vigorously with King Richard against the sequestration of Henry Bolingborke's Lancastrian estates that he ordered their arrest. Warned by the Earl of Worcester what was impending and of the King's intention to send them to the Tower, they hurriedly left for Alnwick and Warkworth where they reunited under arms, surrounded by their feudal retainers. When summoned to appear before the King by a special messenger they excused themselves, pleading that the state of the border did not permit them to leave Northumberland. The King of Scotland offered them hospitality over the border, but for the time being they preferred to remain on their estates.

Among the primary sources for Richard's expedition to Ireland was the account in elegantly written rhymed verses[1] of Jean Créton, the French esquire, who accompanied the Earl of Salisbury to Ireland in search of adventure, merriment and song. He was a lover of music, being especially skilled as a player on the harp. Among the valuable and curious illustrations of Harleian MSS 1319 is a scene showing the author Créton paying his respects to a Gascoigne knight, who he tells us requested him to travel from Paris to London, and thence set out for Ireland to attend King Richard, whose purpose was to subdue the great Irish rebels. All was gaiety in Milford Haven, the town resounding to the music of minstrels and trumpeters as Richard's fleet of two hundred sail took advantage of a favourable wind to leave the port for Ireland. Créton became absolutely devoted to King Richard, describing enthusiastically his many amiable qualities and accomplishments, among which he mentions his genius for poetry and composing chansons and rondeaux. As an eye witness, Créton's account is of considerable value while the King was in Ireland, though too uncritical. He describes Richard sharing the privations of his army and as one who knew how to lead.

The army, consisting of a large number of archers and men-at-arms, landed at Waterford on June 1st, but after waiting for six days for the Duke of Albemarle, marched to Kilkenny where that nobleman at last arrived after two weeks. According to Créton, the the King's cousin now began to behave "in an evil and strange manner". Already at Waterford, Albemarle's behaviour had seemed highly suspicious. Creton describes him as: "That shifty Duke whose guile for ever hid the harm he did."

Among Richard's hostages were Henry of Monmouth, eldest son of Bolingbroke, then a boy hardly twelve, Henry Beaufort and Humphrey of Gloucester, son of his murdered uncle. Créton relates that during the campaign, Richard created Henry of Monmouth a Knight saying, "My fair young cousin, henceforward be *preux* (valiant), for unless you conquer you will have little name for valour." The illumination of folio 5[2] mentions that King Richard conferred with great marks of kindness the Order of Knighthood on the son of Henry, Duke of Lancaster, afterwards Henry V. The young Henry certainly seems to have fallen under the spell of Richard's personality.

As the English army advanced uneasily through the Wicklow mountains, they were confronted by the superb guerrilla tactics of the rebel leader Art MacMurrough, King of Leinster, who avoided pitched battles and ambushed hostile parties of English whenever possible. An illustration (folio 7)[3] depicts the hardships and difficulties faced by Richard's army. On the arrival of three ships containing fresh supplies, the soldiers eagerly ran into the water to get bread. Some of them had not eaten bread for five days.

When MacMurrough demanded an unconditional peace, Richard in Dublin flew into a temper, but it was decided that young Thomas Despenser, Earl of Gloucester, should negotiate with the Irish rebel leader "in some unnamed glen". There is a well known description of this scene (folio 9) where MacMurrough is shown coming forth from between two woods to meet the Earl of Gloucester, described as the King's Commander-in-Chief. A conference then ensues. The Irish are here described as riding without saddles and stirrups. Créton, who was present, describes MacMurrough as a magnificent horseman.

As Richard's army marched through the Wicklow Mountains towards the end of June, Bolingbroke sailed from Vannes in Brittany accompanied by a few close friends and about three hundred men, many of them unarmed, asserting that he merely wished to claim his rightful Lancastrian inheritance. In his party were the ex-Archbishop Arundel, young Thomas Arundel, son of the executed Earl, Sir Thomas Erpingham[4] and various knights and squires. According to Créton, bad weather conditions prevented the news of Henry's sailing from reaching Ireland. Bolingbroke, shrewdly calculating, reckoned whilst in France that thousands of his friends and supporters would join his cause in England. After sailing up and down the south and east coasts, probably to sound the opinions of the people, Henry landed at Ravenspur at the mouth of the Humber between Bridlington and Hull about July 4th.[5] Curiously enough, it was exactly the same place where Edward Duke of York landed in 1471 before becoming Edward IV. Henry wisely made for his own Lancastrian strongholds, Pickering Castle, Knaresborough and Pontefract, which surrendered to him without much resistance. Pontefract proved the main rallying point, for it was here that the Earl of Northumberland and Harry Hotspur, Lord

Willoughby, the Earl of Westmoreland, and a large number of their retainers joined the armed rebellion.

Henry, Duke of Lancaster, was a born propagandist, cunning and absolutely unscrupulous. He immediately sent letters to the remaining prelates, the lords, and the leading citizens, "falsely railing, by different, artful fabrications against King Richard and his government".[6] He told all manner of lies, that the King was plotting the sale of Guyenne and Gascony for private gain, and "that he would keep the villeins of England in greater subjection and harder bondage than any Christian King had ever held his subjects". He claimed that the King intended to put to death all the chief magistrates who opposed him. He even revived the mendacious story that Edmund Crouchback was in reality the elder brother of Edward I and had only been set aside because of his deformities. He wanted the credulous people to believe that Richard's title to the throne was invalid.

Rumours are often evil. All sorts of false rumours abounded in England while Richard was in Ireland, devoid of all truth. *The annales*[7] reported as fact that Richard never intended to return, but to rule England autocratically as a military monarchy based on Cheshire, Wales and Ireland. Nobody any longer could have any security with his property, for it could be wrested from him either by the King or by his Treasurer, the Earl of Wiltshire (William Scrope). By the time Henry reached Doncaster, thirty thousand men had rallied to his side, but to the Percies, Bolingbroke swore a solemn oath that he came to claim his rightful inheritance, not to usurp the throne.[8] Of course he may have been sincere, but it is more than likely that Henry, a born dissembler, hid his secret designs even when banished to France. An able political opportunist, he sensed that developments now favoured him, and with his military astuteness he could use to his own advantage further moves. He instinctively adapted himself to the moment, once he set foot on English soil. So, to say, as does a distinguished Shakespearean scholar, Dr. Dover Wilson, that Bolingbroke "was a man who appears to be borne upwards by a power beyond his volition" is interesting, but unconvincing, for he seems to imply that his motives were lofty and that he was incapable of subterfuge and baseness.

The Regent, Duke of York, might have acted at first with a sense of purposefulness, sending Sir William Bagot to Ireland to warn his nephew of Henry's landing, but he was no soldier and unable to rouse any enthusiasm in the troops especially as most of them believed the Duke of Lancaster had come to claim what was rightfully his own, his titles and lands. A few of Richard's friends, including Henry Despenser, the fighting Bishop of Norwich, and Sir William Elmham showed some signs of resistance, but most of York's men deserted to Lancaster, to be followed by the supine Regent himself. When making his peace with York, the Duke of Lancaster said: "Good uncle, you are right welcome and all your people." Another prominent nobleman, swift to desert Richard for Henry, his half-brother, was John Beaufort, Marquis of Dorset, eldest son of John of Gaunt by Katherine Swynford.

Meanwhile, three of Richard's loyal friends, the Treasurer Scrope, Bushy and Green, sought refuge in Bristol Castle only to be handed over by the Governor Sir Peter Courtenay, who made no show of resistance whatsoever. They were beheaded without trial.

When Sir William Bagot arrived in Dublin, about July 10th, with the intelligence that Henry of Lancaster had invaded the north of England, Richard could not conceal his fury. He favoured an immediate return to North Wales, while the majority of the Council wanted Salisbury to return at once to raise an army in Cheshire and North Wales. According to Créton,[9] the sly and treacherous Albemarle was responsible for persuading King Richard to delay his departure. He went to the King in great secrecy, saying: "Sire, do not vex yourself, for never did I hear a matter so belied. Be not in such haste, now to set out; it were much better to take good time and send for the whole of the navy." It was true that there was insufficient shipping in Dublin, but Richard's departure was delayed from Waterford and he only arrived in Milford Haven about July 25th. Meanwhile the loyal Salisbury, whom his friend the writer, Christina de Pisan, called "Gracieux Chevalier" had landed in North Wales. In his entourage was Jean Créton, who had been persuaded to go with him "for the sake of merriment and song", but to our loss, for we have no eye witness for Richard's return from Waterford eighteen days after Salisbury.

On landing at Milford Haven, Richard is said to have disguised himself in a priest's cowl. To his great dismay, he found that disloyalty was rife in his army, for the Duke of Albemarle and the Earl of Worcester both openly deserted their King. Walsingham maintains that the King ordered his Lord Stewart Worcester to dismiss his household, while Froissart alleges that Sir Thomas Percy broke his white staff, having been commanded by Richard to do so. It is probable that he resented the King calling his brother Northumberland and his nephew, Hotspur, traitors; but he was to atone for the desertion of his master three years later in his noble death, fighting against Henry IV at Shrewsbury. The position at this point for Richard was certainly dangerous, but not desperate. He knew now for certain of the triumphal progress of his cousin now at Bristol with a powerful army, of the execution of some of his friends and counsellors and of the desertion of the Regent York, his uncle.

The Lancastrian legend, intended to denigrate Richard, and to depict him as a frightened King almost bereft of his wits, is a travesty of the truth. According to Créton, Richard was "pale with anger". Henry seems remarkably well informed about the King's movements, that he would make at once for North Wales where he could count on many loyal friends. Lancaster, however, was well served by traitors in Ireland and knew when Richard landed in England.

So as to travel lighter, the King abandoned the royal baggage, plate and chapel furniture and after a hard, hazardous journey of about one hundred and sixty miles along the Welsh coast, travelling through Carmarthen, Harlech, Carnarvon and Beaumaris in Anglesey arrived at Conway, the strongest of Edward I's castles, built from 1283 onwards.

Salisbury had not been inactive. At first he had succeeded in organizing a substantial army consisting mainly of Welsh and men of Cheshire, but disheartened by the King's delayed arrival and prolonged absence, they had unfortunately drifted away. On the whole the best contemporary account is in *The Chronique de la Traison*. There were present with Richard his half-brother, the Duke of Exeter, the Earl of Salisbury, four other knights and the King's confidential clerk Richard Maudelyn, who bore such a remarkable likeness to him. It was a doleful scene as Salisbury and the others related to the King that his army had deserted him. Salisbury related how his esquire tranchant (a confidential servant who not only tasted and carved his lord's meat, but carried his banner immediately behind him in war) had told him the evening before of a letter received by the Earl of Westmoreland from Henry of Lancaster, but he did not know its contents.

Two of the King's advisers now gave their master conflicting advice. It might have been better for Richard if he had followed that of the Earl of Salisbury, instead of the Duke of Exeter. According to the French Chronicler, the King when he had retired into a Council chamber after hearing mass and dining, said, "I know that I am betrayed by that bad man (Henry of Lancaster); for God's sake, advise me what is best to be done." Salisbury favoured taking four or five hundred of the best horsemen at nightfall and going to Bordeaux by sea. There the King would be warmly received by the King of France, his father-in-law. "It is better to withdraw a little from an enemy, " urged Salisbury, "than to put one's self in his power." He was supported by Sir William Fereiby, a devoted follower of Richard's and an executor of his will, by Thomas Merke, Bishop of Carlisle, and by Janico d'Artas (D'Artasse), a captain greatly esteemed and very honourable by nature. He was a Gascon.

It was, however, Exeter who had most influence with his half-brother the King at this juncture, advising him to stay at his Castle of Bellincardie (Beaumaris*), where he might be more secure. "By St. George!" urged Exeter, always ready for a fight, but lacking judgement, "I beg you, my Lord, be ruled by me." The King first said they would be as secure in Bordeaux. Exeter argued that if Richard went to Bordeaux, everybody would say that he had "fled without having been pursued, and that the King must be guilty of some crime or he would have stayed". Far better to remain at Bellincardie Castle where despite Henry of Lancaster and his friends, the King could put to sea if he chose. Besides, while at Bellincardie he might come to an understanding with Henry.

It is completely untrue, as Bishop Stubbs alleges, that "Richard saw at once that all was over and made no attempt to stem the tide of desertion and ingratitude". After a conference held at

* Beaumaris is on the island of Anglesey.

149

Conway, he offered to resign the Crown.[10] As Miss M.V. Clarke argues in her scholarly work: "This rapid slurring over the decisive moment in the revolution reflects the attitude of the official Lancastrian apologists, the St. Albans Chronicler and Adam of Usk,"[11] The testimony of the Parliament Roll can by no means be relied on, for it is a later gross fabrication by Henry IV for purposes of state. Such is the view in 1846 of Benjamin Williams, the editor of *La Traison et Mort*. The Parliament Roll, he writes, "must be branded with fabrication". Wallon, Richard's nineteenth century French biographer, is correct when he writes that "la fausseté de l'abdication de Richard à Conway est prouvée". Shakespeare as a great artist and dramatist relied mainly on the Lancastrian Chronicles, and his picture of Richard at Flint Castle (he does not mention Conway) as a hysterical, demented King meekly yielding his Crown to Henry is a false one. Richard, with his absolute belief and faith in his *regalitée*, and in the anointment ritual, always adhered to the view that nobody could deprive him of these sacred and priceless assets. Shakespeare wrote:

> No water in the rough, rude sea,
> Can wash the balm from an anointed King.

Richard could have fled overseas or even stayed for a long period in one of his impregnable Welsh castles, but he was lured from Conway Castle by the despicable cunning and political finesse of Henry of Lancaster and betrayed by Northumberland and Archbishop Arundel into his hands.

At first Richard sent Exeter and his nephew Surrey (the account in *La Traison* does not mention Surrey) on an embassy to Henry of Lancaster, with an authority from the King to offer him his lands and titles, but to ask him what further he wanted and why he continued his open rebellion. Henry was in Chester, having recently executed one of Richard's most faithful and trusty friends, Sir Peers à Legh, of Lyme, commonly called Perkyn à Lee,[12] a member of an ancient Cheshire family. Henry commanded that Perkyn à Lee's head be set up on one of the highest turrets in the Eastgate "aboute all the citie". Exeter was related to Henry as well as Richard, for he had married Elizabeth, a daughter of John of

Gaunt many years before. Henry of Lancaster refused to answer, insisted on keeping Exeter and Surrey hostages and forced both noblemen to give up King Richard's cognizances or badges of the White Hart.[13] Despite his earlier protestations to the contrary, it would seem likely that Henry was now determined to seize Richard's Crown. According to the *Chronique de la Traison*, the Duke of Exeter wept when compelled to part with his half-brother's White Hart, but the perfidious Earl of Rutland (Albemarle) who was present said to him, "Good Cousin, do not vex yourself, for please God, things will go well."

Henry sent the Earl of Northumberland and the ex-Archbishop Arundel on a mission to Conway Castle, his object being to get possession of Richard by duplicity or force. What actually transpired was one of the most despicable acts of betrayal in the history of our country. The *Chronique de la Traison* only mentions Northumberland as an envoy, but most of the other chroniclers, for instance, Adam of Usk, include Arundel. Among the beautiful illustrations in Harleian 1319 is one of Richard II receiving the elderly nobleman now aged fifty-seven, dressed in a robe of blue dotted with gold stars. Far from showing any sign of disrespect (as Shakespeare says), Northumberland is making obeisance to his King. Actually Henry Percy may well have believed the Duke of Lancaster's protestations at Doncaster, including his solemn oath, that he had no designs on the throne. The weight of evidence is against Northumberland having agreed before his interview with Richard to any plan by Henry of Lancaster of claiming the throne.[14] Nevertheless, Northumberland was guilty of a gross act of perjury in Conway Castle. Obviously with the intention of deceiving Richard, Henry's envoys took with them four hundred lancers and one thousand archers. Most of these men were cunningly set in ambush in the mountains between Conway and Rhuddlan. Only a small delegation actually came to Conway Castle.

The terms offered by Northumberland were reasonable enough if they had been sincere. Richard might keep his throne, provided he agreed to restore Henry's lands and right his wrongs and that he may be seneschal "grand juge of England as his father and his predecessors have been". Actually Henry had not waited for Richard's sanction, but already assumed this office. Richard must declare for

151

a free Parliament, and agree to surrender to Henry, Exeter, Surrey, the Bishop of Carlisle, and his personal clerk Maudeleyn. Far from behaving in a neurotic fashion or as a coward, the King had difficulty in concealing his anger. He told Northumberland that he needed time to consider the negotiations.

Withdrawing to a council chamber with his friends Salisbury, Fereiby*, Sir Stephen Scrope, the Bishop of Carlisle and the Gascon squire Janico d'Artas, the King said: "Whatever agreement or peace Henry of Lancaster may make with me, if I can ever get him into my power, I will cause him to be foully put to death, just as he hath deserved."[15] Other accounts allege that Richard threatened that as soon as fortune turned in his favour, "he would flay some people alive". Richard's demeanour at Conway is not that of a King with the slightest intention of abdicating his throne. When Richard and his friends were in the chapel of the Castle, Thomas Merke of Carlisle made the sensible suggestion that the Earl of Northumberland should be made to swear a solemn oath "on the body of our Lord" that his message from Henry of Lancaster was the truth. The writer of the *Chronique de la Traison* compares Northumberland with Judas or Guenelon, a traitor who was torn into pieces at Aix-la-Chapelle by order of Charlemagne.

One can imagine the austere scene in the dim candlelight of the chapel, the strained faces of Richard and the noblemen as mass was chanted and Northumberland made his solemn oath, to the medieval mind much more solemn than any treaty. After they had dined, this passed between the King and the Earl. "Northumberland, for God's sake be sure you consider well what you have sworn, for it will be to your damnation if it be untrue."[16] "Dear Sire," replied Northumberland, "if you find it untrue, treat me as you ought a traitor." In such a way was Richard betrayed, persuaded to go to Flint to be delivered into Henry of Lancaster's hands. On the pretext of going on ahead to order the King's supper, the Earl of Northumberland left Conway.

It cannot be true that Richard was easy in his mind or altogether unsuspecting of the evil that would follow as he rode with about twenty of his friends and attendants in the direction of Rhuddlan. Northumberland had returned to his men under Sir Thomas Erpingham, who lay in ambush in the wild mountain

* William Fereiby, consistently loyal to King Richard; one of his executors, later involved in a plot against Henry IV and executed.

passes. He told them to be merry, for they would soon have what they wanted.

About six miles from the banks of the Conway (Convy) the coastal path passes over the wild and rocky headland of Penmaeurhos. Here the King was forced to dismount. He was descending on foot when with a gasp of horror he saw the sharp glint of steel. "I am betrayed. God of paradise assist me," he cried. "Do you not see below banners and streamers?" he exclaimed to the Earl of Salisbury. "Certainly, Sire, I do," said that nobleman, "and my heart is full of foreboding." The Bishop of Carlisle said that he strongly suspected that man had betrayed him. When Northumberland approached Richard with twelve others, the King said, reproachfully, "Northumberland, if I thought you intended to betray me, I would return to Conway." Placing his hand on Richard's bridle, the Earl exclaimed, "By St. George, my lord, you shall not return for this month to come, for I shall conduct you to the Duke of Lancaster as I have promised him."[17] Just then the trumpets sounded and Sir Thomas Erpingham approached with Northumberland's men. Students of Shakespeare will remember him as Henry V's good old knight at Agincourt, but to Richard's devoted partisans he later proved sadistic and cruel. Northumberland afterwards denied any involvement to make Henry of Lancaster King.[18] but he was certainly deeply implicated in the despicable plot which made it possible for Henry to achieve this ambition.

Sorrowfully and full of lamentation the King and his companions, now in effect Northumberland's prisoners, were borne to Flint Castle where he and Erpingham placed a strong guard over them. Together with five horsemen, the Earl immediately rode to Chester to apprize the Duke of Lancaster of the King's capture. Flint is only a short distance from Chester, a matter of ten miles. The *Kirkstall Chronicle* relates that it was Henry, not Northumberland, who treated Richard as a captive once he had been brought to Flint. Certainly it was tragic for Richard to stand upon the castle walls and to see his cousin's army in their armour shining in the morning sun marching along the beach. The *Chronique de la Traison* account relates Henry's interview with Richard in Flint Castle. "Fair cousin of Lancaster, ye are right welcome," said Richard, and what it must have cost him. Lancaster replied, "My

Lord, I am come before you sent me," accusing the King of having governed the kingdom badly. The Monk of Evesham, however, does not mention Henry's complaint. Apparently Duke Henry conversed with the Bishop of Carlisle, but refused to talk to the Earl of Salisbury, remembering the disdainful way that nobleman had treated him in Paris. The *Annales* relate that Richard was treated by Henry *'reverenter et honeste'*, but that is not the impression given by Créton, an eyewitness at Flint and on the journey to Chester and London.

If Richard had not taken the cream of his royal bodyguard and of the men of Chester, nine hundred archers, one hundred and ten men-at-arms, and various knights to Ireland[19] - surely a tragic mistake - they might have stubbornly resisted Henry of Lancaster. Despite the devotion of the men of the principality to Richard, Chester fell too easily into Henry's hands. By August 14th (1399), Hotspur had been appointed Justice for Chester "for his most dread lord Henry Duke of Lancaster and Steward of England". Hotspur gave strict orders for the preservation of peace within Cheshire under his personal seal, the official seal having been removed to Wales.[20] In an analysis of the causes of Richard's downfall, the King's too great dependence on Cheshire must be stressed. The Cheshire archers had once boasted, according to Walsingham, that they would protect Richard, *"contra totum Angliam . . . , immo, contra totum mundum"*.

The King was imprisoned for the time being in the donjon of Chester Castle on August 19th, and much to his sorrow separated from his dearest friends, the Earl of Salisbury and the Bishop of Carlisle. On the same day, Duke Henry issued writs in King Richard's name for a Parliament to assemble at Westminster on September 30th.

On August 25th the Duke of Lancaster and his army set off, taking the King with them to London. Passing through Lichfield there was an attempt to rescue him, probably by a mixed band of Welshmen and men of Chester, but it failed. From that time onward "he was guarded as strickly as a thief or a murderer".[21] Créton says that he was most shamefully treated. The Welsh, however, gave Henry plenty of trouble, killing the English whenever they could and stripping them without mercy. At Coventry they re-

154

mained three days. According to Créton, on the march through the Midlands, six or seven notable burgesses of London came to meet Duke Henry, humbly beseeching him to behead King Richard. Henry told them that he would do nothing of the kind, but he would bring him to London where Parliament would decide what was to be done to him. In London, Henry left Richard to be guarded by two of his enemies, Gloucester and Arundel.

Meanwhile the Duke of Lancaster enjoyed his own triumphal entry into the City of London, through Ludgate to St. Paul's where, on seeing his father's tomb, he wept exceedingly. There was much shouting, and the cry arose: "Long live the Duke of Lancaster." "And the bells of the churches and monasteries rang so merrily," ironically wrote the French author of *La Traison*, "that you could not hear God thundering." The King, however, clothed in a plain black gown and riding a tiny nag was taken to the Palace of Westminster where he passed the night. On the morrow, very early, he heard mass for the last time in Westminster Abbey. Henry's propaganda had certainly borne fruit among the Londoners. We are told that some cursed him loudly, saying: "Now we are well revenged on this wicked bastard who has governed us so ill." Others merely pitied him. In this ignominious manner, Richard was borne to the Tower of London.

From September 2nd 1399 for one month, there was no effective head of state in England, though all proclamations and statutes were published in King Richard's name. The accounts from French sources do not refer to a craven King Richard in the Tower. He remained dignified and regal in adversity. When the Duke of Lancaster gave a message to the young Earl of Arundel that King Richard should visit him, he was curtly told that he would only speak to him if Lancaster came to him. A terrible scene occurred in the Tower where Richard charged his uncle the Duke of York and his son Albemarle (Rutland) with treason. He is alleged to have said to Rutland, "Thou, and the villein thy father, have both of you foully betrayed me. I pray to God, and to St. John the Baptist, that cursed may be the hour wherein ye were born." Thus he spoke to the cousin who had once been his dearest friend. Of Henry of Lancaster he demanded, "Why do you keep me so closely guarded by your men-at-arms? Do you acknowledge me as your lord and king or what do you mean to to with me?"[22] Duke Henry replied that Richard was his lord and King, but that the Council of the realm had ordered him to be kept in confinement until Parliament met. In all fairness to Henry of Lancaster, he showed Richard all possible respect at this interview. It seems the height of cruelty, however, for the King to have been denied the solace of the company of his little Queen Isabelle when he asked to see her. Above all, the King felt the humiliation of his position, "for he was a loyal knight and I never forfeited my knighthood". What makes the French sources more convincing is that they are for the most part substantiated by the Chronicle written early in the fifteenth century in the Cistercian Abbey of Dieulacres, a house owning property in both Cheshire and Staffordshire. Since it was far enough away from Westminster the monks dared to record a fair account.

Henry based his claim to Richard's throne firstly, on hereditary descent and, secondly, on conquest. His problem was to make a convincing case, not based on flimsy theory, but on solid fact. Henry's hereditary claim was based on the legend that he was in reality the true heir descended from Edmund Crouchback, supposed second son of Henry III, who had been passed over for the succession to the throne because of his deformity in favour of his younger brother Edward. Henry always maintained his "right descent from Henry III". If there was truth in the legend, the first three Edwards were not legitimate kings, but Henry of Lancaster was rightful king through his mother Blanche of Lancaster (John of Gaunt's first wife).[23] It was unfortunate for Henry that no real evidence existed to support the truth of that allegation. When Henry appointed a commission of "sages in the law", including the Lancastrian Chronicler Adam of Usk, to weigh the evidence in the various monasteries, their report was entirely negative, for they could give Henry no support for his hereditary claim. Actually a little boy aged eight, Edmund Mortimer, Earl of March, heir of Roger killed in Ireland, had a more valid claim to the throne than Henry, assuming that Roger had been approved by Parliament in 1385 as Richard's heir presumptive. Edmund was directly descended from Philippa, daughter of Lionel of Clarence, Edward III's third son. England, however, had had enough of little boys succeeding to the throne. It is interesting that Edmund's aunt, Elizabeth, was the wife of Harry Hotspur (Percy), lending substance to the belief that he never willingly acquiesced in Henry IV's usurpation of Richard's throne.

When discarding the Crouchback legend, the commission of "sages in the law" in their report stated that Richard's "perjories, sacrileges, unnatural armies, exactions from his subjects, reduction of his people to slavery, cowardice, and weakness of rule" were sufficient causes for his deposition.

What was grossly unfair to Richard - and he protested at it - was that he was never allowed a trial or to appear in person to present his case and to rebut the accusations of his enemies. The *Dieulacres Chronicle* mentions the King's demand for a public trial.

Archbishop Walden had now been deprived of the Archbishopric of Canterbury, though later compensated with the Bishopric of London through the influence of Henry's friend Archbishop Arundel, now restored to his former position as Archbishop of Canterbury. Arundel exercised a great deal of influence before King Richard's deposition. He certainly wanted Henry King on his own terms. Instead of the Duke of Lancaster advancing hereditary claims - insubstantial as they were - he favoured Richard, if possible, nominating Henry as his heir, followed by his willing abdication. Henry would then ascend the throne as his cousin's legal successor, but Parliament would control his kingship. Such a plan did not take into account Richard's natural reluctance to surrender his *regalitée*, the mysterious essence of kingship conferred upon him as a boy during the anointing ceremony at his Coronation. It had been given him by God, and Richard believed that it would be wrongful for him to renounce it.

XII   Deposition

The tragic story moved rapidly to its culmination. One thing is clear. The official version invented by the supporters of Henry of Lancaster and recorded in the Rolls of Parliament that the King cheerfully resigned his crown is false. Nor is it true that he agreed to abdicate his throne in Conway Castle. The Lancastrian sympathizer, Adam of Usk, was present in the Tower on September 21st when Richard was dining, and gives a convincing and sympathetic account of how the King reflected about his misfortunes. He wrote:

> And there and then the King discoursed sorrowfully in these words, "My God: a wonderful land is this, and a fickle - which hath exiled, slain, destroyed, or ruined so many kings, rulers and great men, and is ever tainted and toileth with strife and variance and envy . . . " Perceiving then the trouble of his mind and how that none of his own men, nor such as were wont to serve him, but strangers who were but spies upon him, were appointed to his service, and musing on his ancient and wonted glory and on the fickle fortune of the world, I departed thence much moved at heart.[1]

It is a passage which inspired Shakespeare to write great poetry.[2]

Richard certainly does not give the impression of being insane while he was in confinement. Clearly during the last two years of his reign he had made fatal misjudgements both as to people and as to events. Unfortunately he became curiously insensitive to the wider political consequences of his actions. When Richard pleaded again and again for a fair trial, Henry merely said, "My Lord, be not afraid, nothing unreasonable shall be done to you." It is probable that Richard never resigned his throne to Henry, but only to God as the *Dieulacres Chronicle* maintains.

158

On September 30th 1399 a large, excited assembly consisting of representatives of the "estates of Parliament" and many London citizens gathered in the Palace of Westminster. It cannot be constitutionally called a Parliament, for the King was not present, nor was there the customary opening speech of the Chancellor or the appointment of a Speaker. At this historic assembly, Richard's renunciation was read in Latin to the assembly, and the thirty-two charges or so-called 'gravamina'. One of the main accusations was that he had violated his coronation oath, and had ruled according to his will, instead of accepting the laws and customs of the country. These charges are contained in the *Annales Ricardi II et Henrici IV*.[3] By squandering his possession Richard had enforced grievous burdens on his people by taxation. He was accused of saying "that the laws were in his own mouth, and frequently in his own breast and that only he himself could change and make the laws of the realm". There were many other offences, such as wrongfully exiling Archbishop Arundel and deceiving him, so that he never attended the Parliament which condemned him to exile. There were the more serious accusations such as the employment of forced oaths, the tampering with justice, and the use of blank charters for further exactions from his subjects. There is one curious omission, only one mention in the "gravamina" of Richard's duplicity in foreign affairs. The real truth is that his enemies could find little to criticize in Richard's handling of foreign affairs. The evidence is far from satisfactory that his foreign policy was intended to promote a domestic tyranny at home.[4] In all fairness to Richard, he had shown high intelligence in his negotiations with foreign powers. He never sacrificed vital English interests abroad.

Having heard these charges, "the estates of the realm" pronounced that there was enough proof in the "gravamina" and concurred that Richard should be deposed. It was said that he "was utterly unworthy and useless to rule and govern the realm".

In claiming the throne, Henry of Lancaster was the first medieval King to speak in English, the *lingua materna*. He said: "In the name of Fadir, Son and Holy Gost, I Henry of Lancastr chalenge yis Rewyne of England and the Corone." Henry based his claim on his descent "fro the gude lorde kynge Henry therde".[5]

Both Chief Justice Thirnyng and Archbishop Arundel had objected to Henry claiming the crown by right of conquest. Thirnyng and Arundel were responsible for preparing the "gravamina", the accusations against Richard. After Henry had been enthroned by the Archbishops of Canterbury and York, Arundel preached a sermon, warning Henry to rule well and wisely and to be guided by Parliament. Through the dim mazes of the revolution the principle of the sovereignty of Parliament seemed to emerge.

The *Chronique de la Traison* is the main authority for the courageous protest of Thomas Merke, the Bishop of Carlisle, against these proceedings. It is probable that there were other disentient voices. The Bishop's speech was deeply impressive:

> My lords, consider well before you give judgement upon what my lord the Duke has set forth, for I maintain that there is not one present who is competent and fit to judge such a sovereign as my lord the King whom we have acknowledged our lord for the space of twenty years and more, and I will give you my reasons; there never was, nor is in this world, any false traitor, nor wicked murderer, who, if he be taken prisoner by the hands of justice, is not at the least, brought before the judge to hear his sentence. My lords, you have well and truly heard the accusations that my lord the Duke has made against King Richard; and it appears to me that you are about to give judgement and to condemn King Richard, without hearing what he has to answer, or even his being present. Moreover, I say that my lord the Duke was banished ten years by the Council of the realm, and by the consent of his own father, for the great crime which he and the Duke of Norfolk committed; and he has returned to the country without the King's permission: and moreover, I say he has done still worse, for he has seated himself on the throne, where no lord ought to sit other than the lawfully crowned King of England; wherefore I declare that you ought to bring King Richard in presence of the full Parliament to hear what he has to say, and to see whether he be willing to relinquish his crown to the Duke or not.[6]

Merke was immediately placed in the custody of the Abbot of St. Albans, deprived of his bishopric, and later committed to the Tower (January 1400), but eventually pardoned by Henry IV. He became Rector of Todenham in Gloucestershire and died in 1409.

On the following day, Sir Richard of Bordeaux was visited by Sir William Thirnyng and the proctors of the estates to inform him of the act of deposition and that they had renounced their allegiance. Richard then said, pathetically, "I hope that myn cosyn wold be good lord to me". He remained obdurate to the end, maintaining to the Chief Justice that he could not renounce the spiritual authority imparted to him at his Coronation. Thirnyng rejected his plea, saying that Richard had already owned that he was unworthy to reign.

The Kirkstall Chronicle says that Richard owed his wretched plight to the fact that he had spurned the advice of the greater dukes, and senior lords and relied too readily on the young lords and others, "completely inexperienced in weighty decisions". However, this Chronicle is a classic example of a monkish chronicler adapting his political stance according to the changed circumstances of the day. No doubt it was prudent now to call Thomas Arundel Archbishop of Canterbury "an exceptionally wise man" and to refer to the worthy (*venerabilis*) Earl of Arundel.

The usurper Henry IV was crowned in Westminster Abbey on St. Edwards Day, October 13th 1399, a clever day to choose, for it marked the anniversary of the feast of the translation of St. Edward, one of Richard's patron saints. Earlier Henry had created forty-six new knights, including his three younger sons. Henry, his eldest son, had already been knighted by Richard in Ireland. When summoned by his father to return to Chester, the young prince had spent much of the time with Richard for whom he had acquired "a deep affection". He even regarded his father as a traitor. Now he bore the sword 'Curtana' at the Coronation. It was fortunate for Henry that the sacred oil of Edward the Confessor was used during the anointing ceremony, but it was found that the new King's head was full of lice. According to Adam of Usk, during the offertory, Henry dropped a gold noble, later picked up by the

Chronicler. Although the Earl of Northumberland played a conspicuous part, bearing the first sword, his son Harry 'Hotspur' refused to attend the Coronation banquet, according to the *Dieulacres Chronicle*. Four years later Hotspur was to die on the field of Shrewsbury, fighting desperately against Henry IV.

As for Sir Richard of Bordeaux, disguised as a forester, he was taken from the Tower on October 28th by boat, then borne to Leeds Castle in Kent under the custody of John Pelham. A poignant experience for the deposed King because of its happy memories. Adam of Usk relates that Richard when carried away on the Thames in the silence of dark midnight, wept bitterly, loudly lamenting that he had ever been born. From Leeds he was taken to Pontefract Castle where Robert de Waterton, a staunch supporter of Henry IV, was governor. Both Froissart and Adam of Usk give different earlier accounts how the former King's greyhound called Math, who followed him everywhere, deserted Richard for Henry, sensing instinctively Lancaster's triumph.

Henry's great problem was what to do with the deposed King. Provided that his cousin was securely kept in imprisonment in perpetuity at Pontefract, whose custodian was his own half-brother Sir Thomas Swynford, Henry was for the present satisfied. However, there were many about him - Councillors, Londoners, and members of Parliament - only too ready to remind the King that he could not enjoy any security while Richard lived, but he turned a deaf ear to their entreaties. Only if an armed rising was to occur would Richard be the first to die. Henry's conscience would never give him peace of mind.[7]

He spent his first Christmas as King in Windsor Castle, but Richard's friends, Despenser (he had been deprived of the earldom of Gloucester), Huntingdon (no longer Duke of Exeter), Kent (formerly Duke of Surrey), and the faithful Salisbury, conspired with Colchester, the Abbot of Westminster[8] and Sir Thomas Blount. They were involved in a desperate conspiracy against the Usurper King. It is surely difficult to understand, bearing in mind Albemarle's (now Earl of Rutland) treachery, why the conspirators confided in him at all. Their plan was to storm Windsor Castle and to kill or capture King Henry and his eldest son.[9] It was at Kingston-on-Thames where the conspirators collected, having already arranged through a confederate that Windsor Castle should be betrayed into their hands. It was proposed that Maudelyn, who strongly resembled the former King, should impersonate his master until Richard could be released from Pontefract Castle.

Among minor conspirators were Sir Bernard Brocas, a Gascon knight, who had held high office at the Court of Richard II and Anne of Bohemia, a landowner in Berkshire and probable owner of the Brocas Meads at Eton.[10] He was later beheaded.

The French authorities, including *La Traison*, relate that the plot was betrayed to Rutland's father, the Duke of York, by his son and then to the new King himself.[11] Henry escaped to London, together with his sons, where he was apprized of the danger by the Mayor. According to Hall, Henry reached the capital at twelve o'clock at night. The Mayor brought him reinforcements of three thousand archers and three thousand bill-men. Henry, a brilliant organizer, soon assembled an army of twenty thousand men.

Meanwhile, the conspirators entered Windsor Castle, only to find their intended victim had got away. On the following day, they rode to the Palace of Sonning, now no more, where the child-Queen Isabelle, griefstricken for her husband, was residing. After swearing undying loyalty to Isabelle, the conspirators decided to make for the west. By now they had heard of Henry's superior forces who were in hot pursuit. The Earl of Kent (Thomas Holland) fought courageously on Maidenhead bridge, holding up the advance of Henry's vanguard and capturing two pack-horses, two baggage wagons and a chariot of the King's.

Kent, Salisbury and other supporters of the former King passed a night at an inn in Cirencester, while their army found quarters in the surrounding countryside. The *Chronique de la Traison* gives a detailed circumstantial account of events. The sympathies of the townsfolk were with Henry rather than with Richard. During the night an armed mob surrounded the inn, and seized both Kent and Salisbury. They were made prisoners, according to Walsingham and dragged out to the marketplace where they were executed, no doubt brutally treated in the process. The account in *La Traison* is rather different. Kent is said to have been killed by a flight of arrows while fighting, and Salisbury was also overpowered and slain. Kent, only twenty-five at this time, a gallant nobleman, was much loved by his uncle King Richard, who left him £10,000 in his will. The loyal Salisbury, brave soldier, poet, scholar, and by conviction a Lollard, refused the ministrations of a priest as he prepared to die, preferring his own prayers.[1 2]

Richard's half-brother, Huntingdon, fled to Essex, whilst attempting to escape overseas, only to fall into the hands of the vindictive Countess of Hereford, mother-in-law of Henry IV and sister of the beheaded Earl of Arundel. The Countess of Hereford must have resented Huntingdon's harsh treatment of the young Arundel while his prisoner. When her retainers showed some reluctance to execute Huntingdon, the enraged lady said: "Cursed be ye all ye villeins? Have you not courage enough amongst you all to put a man to death?" He was dragged to Pleshy Castle and executed there.

Another of Richard's friends, Thomas Despenser, after escaping over the roofs of houses in Cirencester, reached his own Castle of Cardiff, to be captured and meet the same fate in Bristol.

How cruel and savage were those medieval times! Under the most vile torture, Sir Thomas Blount remained loyal and constant to Richard. When asked to confess the names of his associates in treason, Sir Thomas said not a word, so Sir Thomas Erpingham taunted him saying, "Now go and seek a master who will cure you." His bloody head was sent to decorate London Bridge. Henry V's gallant old knight at Agincourt had grisly streaks in his character.

In sparing the life of John Ferrour, however, Henry IV showed he was not ungrateful to the man who had once saved his own life from the mob who were thirsting for the blood of Archbishop Sudbury eighteen years before.

Epilogue

The insurrection of Sir Richard of Bordeaux's friends signified that his own death would surely follow.

"God alone knows the truth of the manner of his death, a little after the feast of purification of the glorious Virgin (February 2nd 1400)," wrote the Kirkstall Abbey Chronicler. A mystery clings to it even today. The most probable cause of Richard's death was his forcible starvation by his gaolers in Pontefract Castle. There is certainly a ring of truth in Adam of Usk's statement that he perished heartbroken "tormented by Sir Thomas Swynford with starving fare". The Lancastrians prefer the story that he voluntarily starved to death. One thing is absolutely clear. It was necessary for Richard to die, and Henry, conscience-stricken, was forced to recognize it.

A suspicious Council minute exists suggesting that Henry was responsible for his cousin's murder. It is dated February 8th (1400) and reads:

> If Richard the late King be alive, as it is supposed he is, it be ordered that he be well and surely guarded for the salvation of the state . . . but if he be dead, that then he be openly shown to the people, that they might have knowledge thereof.

It is certain that by St. Valentine's Day almost a week later that the King was dead.

The story in the *Chronique de la Traison* and other French sources is far from convincing. These accounts state that King Richard was slain by Sir Peter Exton, who had been ordered by Henry IV to kill Richard. The former King defended himself bravely when attacked by Exton, but he smote the wretched captive a heavy blow on the head from which he died. If there is any truth in the Exton story, it is curious that Dean Stanley of Westminster examined Richard's skeleton in 1871 and could find no signs of violence.

No doubt King Henry spread abroad the slanderous story, mentioned by Froissart, that Richard was in reality the son of a handsome French clerk or canon in the service of the Black Prince, who had made his mother the Princess Joan pregnant. Just because Richard tended to favour the French and desired peace with them, does not prove anything.

During March the body of the murdered King, splendidly embalmed and enclosed in a coffin, was slowly borne south on its melancholy journey through Cheapside, so familiar to Richard in his days of glory, to St. Paul's. A hundred torch bearers in black attended the funeral hearse. In London a further thirty torch bearers in white followed the coffin. It was intended that 20,000 people could gaze on Richard, to realize that he was indeed dead. The former King was first interred in the Dominican Priory of King's Langley, in Hertfordshire, near the palace where he had once been so happy with his first Queen. Fifteen years later Henry V, mindful of his early affection for the ill-fated King, had his body removed to Westminster Abbey where he lies today in a splendid tomb in the St. Edward Chapel with his beloved Anne.

A legend persisted for many years, however, that Richard was still alive. His double Richard Maudeleyn, Confessor and Secretary, had been executed during the 1400 insurrection, but it was alleged that his body had been substituted for Richard's, an ingenious story, but almost certainly untrue. A tradition mentioned by Wylie (Henry IV's biographer; see his volume I, p. 114) relates that Richard escaped from Pontefract, aided by a priest in Hotspur's service. The deposed King was set upon a horse, taken to Northumberland and afterwards conveyed to Scotland. In 1403 the Percies rebelled against Henry IV, spreading abroad rumours whether they believed them or not that Richard was alive in Cheshire. One of their objects in their manifesto was to restore him to the throne.

Henry was indeed so embarrassed by the revelations of a Franciscan friar from Aylesbury that he had the wretched man hanged in his frock, his head cut off and fastened upon London Bridge. Bower, a Scottish historian, has a fantastic story that Richard managed to escape to the Isles, only to be recognized when sitting in the kitchen of Donald 'Lord of the Isles' by a former jester at Richard's Court. Escorted by Lord Montgomery to Robert III's Court, he was treated with much honour, to die later in Stirling Castle.

Isabelle, Richard's child Queen, pined for her husband, refusing to discard her mourning. Henry IV wanted her to marry the Prince of Wales, but she was inflexible in her rejection of Henry of Monmouth, hating his father as the murderer of her Richard. When she eventually left England to go to her father she showed a countenance of lowering and evil aspect to King Henry, scarcely opening her lips. There was the usual haggling over her jewels and her dowry. Eventually she married Charles of Angoulême, who succeeded to the dukedom of Orleans. Charles VI would never have allowed his daughter to marry if he had believed Richard was alive. A truly tragic life, for Isabelle died in child-birth in the Castle of Blois in 1408.

Today we can recognize Richard as a King, who held bold, imaginative and original ideas of kingship, little understood by his contemporaries. He anticipated some of the later doctrines accepted by the Stuarts of the Divine Right of Kings. Richard was in many ways a highly intelligent man, who pursued an enlightened foreign policy, particularly in his diplomatic relations with France.

Our greatest Queen Elizabeth I as an old lady, in August 1601, confronted with the Essex insurrection, realized the significance and importance of Richard II when she said to William Lambarde, Keeper of the Records: "I am Richard II, know ye not that?" She was alluding to the playing of the *Tragedy of Richard II* at the Globe Theatre. To the first Elizabethans, the grim play bore a strange analogy to the troubled times two hundred years later.

Notes

Chapter I

1. The French called le Prince de Galles, le Prince Noir from the black armour he wore.
2. A rather weak character. Beheaded owing to the machinations of Roger Mortimer, Earl of March, paramour of Queen Isabel, 'she-wolf' of France.
3. See Armitage-Smith's biography of *John of Gaunt*, p. 209. Henry Bolingbroke was his heir.
4. Whether or not Alice Perrers was indeed a vile woman as described by Walsingham is at least uncertain. According to the Chronicler, a priest was the sole witness to the heartless robbing of Edward III's rings on his death-bed, but Walsingham is very prejudiced.
5. *The Liber Regalis*. The illustrations probably painted in 1382 or 1383.
6. See *The Westminster Chronicle* 1381-1384, edited and translated by the late H.C. Hector and Barbara F. Harvey, p. 415.
7. *A Chronicle of the Reigns of Richard II, Henry IV, Henry V and Henry VI*, edited by the Rev. John Silvester Davis.
8. According to *Stow's Survey*. See also *England in the Age of Chaucer* by William Woods, p. 30.
9. *Medieval London* by Sir Walter Besant.
10. *England in the Age of Chaucer* by William Woods.

Chapter II

1. See Sir Arthur Bryant's *Set in a Silver Sea*, p. 302.
2. Wright, *Political Poems and Songs*. Song against the Friars, pp. 263-8.
3. Bryant, *Set in a Silver Sea*.
4. His chapter on *The Peasant Revolt*.
5. *Ibid.*, Froissart.
6. See Green's, *A Short History of the English People*, Vol. I.
7. Especially valuable for contemporary reactions.
8. *Westminster Chronicle* 1381-1384, edited and translated by the late H.C. Hector and Barbara F. Harvey, 1982.
9. According to Froissart.
10. Actually Sudbury had surrendered the Seal into the King's hands on Wednesday June 12th. Two days later, it was entrusted temporarily to the Earl of Arundel. On August 10th when the Court was at Reading Abbey, William Courtenay, Bishop of London, soon to be Archbishop of Canterbury was appointed Chancellor.
11. See also *Richard II in the Early Chronicles* by Louise D. Dals.
12. The site of the present Savoy Hotel.
13. *The Hollow Crown* by Harold F. Hutchison (1961).
14. *The Usurper King* by Marie Louise Bruce (1987), p. 44.

15. The Monk of Westminister says that it was the afternoon.
16. *Knighton's Chronicle II*, 150.
17. Green's *A Short History of the English People*, vol. 2, p. 491.
18. *The Royal Policy of Richard II* by R.H. Jones (1965).
19. *Constitutional History of England*, vol. 2.
20. *The Hollow Crown* by Harold F. Hutchison (1961).
    The Conservative Government are about to impose a poll tax during Mrs. Thatcher's third term.

Chapter III

1. Holinshed's *Chronicle*.
2. *The Court of Richard II* by Gervase Mathew (1968).
3. Her blind grandfather King John of Bohemia, father of Charles IV, had fought heroically at the Battle of Crécy (1346), losing his life fighting for France.
4. *The Court of Richard II*, Mathew.
5. *Anne of Bohemia, Lives of Queens*, Agnes Strickland, Vol. I.
6. Aubrey later became Tenth Earl.
7. *Lectures and Notes on Shakespeare and other poets*.
8. Named Philippa after her maternal grandmother Philippa of Hainault. Born in 1367.
9. Miss M.V. Clarke, *Fourteenth Century Studies*, p. 117.
10. D.N.B., also *Stow's Annals*.
11. See *Richard II*, Act 2, Scene 1.
12. *English Art 1307-1460* by Dr. Joan Evans.
13. *The Usurper King* by Marie Louise Bruce.
14. *English Art 1307-1460*, Evans.
15. Transactions of the Royal Society, Fourth Series (1939). *English and Czech influences on Hussite movement* by Betts.
16. *Ibid*.
17. *The Westminster Chronicle for the Years 1381-94*, edited and translated by L.C. Hector.
18. See L.C. Hector in *English Historical Review*, Vol. LXVIII, 62-65.
19. *The Hollow Crown*, Harold F. Hutchison. *Ibid*. L.C. Hector, *English Historical Review*.
20. Adam of Usk's *Chronicon A.D. 1377-1421*, edited by Sir Edward Maunde Thompson, p. 143.
21. *Ibid*., Adam of Usk.
22. Monk of Westminster.
23. Monk of Westminster.
24. *Lectures and Notes on Shakespeare and other English Poets* by Samuel Taylor Coleridge.
25. *The Hollow Crown*, Hutchison. Monk of Evesham.
26. *Henry IV*, Part I.
27. *Ibid*.
28. Cited by Miss M.V. Clarke, *Fourteenth Century Studies*.
29. *Queens of England*, Agnes Strickland, Vol. I.

Chapter IV

1. *The Portugal Story* by John dos Passos.
2. Act I, Scene 2.
3. £600,000 in modern currency.
4. *England in the Age of Chaucer* by William Woods.
5. *Medieval London*, Vol. I, by Sir Walter Besant.
6. Walsingham gives details of the trial. See also *The Hollow Crown* by Harold Hutchison.
7. The name of the author of this work is by no means certain.
8. *Continuation of Book V of Chronicon Henrici*, Knighton, Vol. II, edited by Rev. Joseph Rawson.
9. Knighton II, 215.
10. Steel's *Richard II*, p. 97.
11. There was no such Statute.
12. *English Historical Review* by N.B. Lewis, pp. 402-407. Also M.V. Clarke's *Fourteenth Century Studies*.
13. *Ibid.*, M.V. Clarke.
14. *Ibid.*, *The Hollow Crown*, Hutchison.
15. *Chronicle of Adam of Usk* (Maunde Thompson), p. 142.
16. D.N.B., *Richard II*.
17. *Set in a Silver Sea*, Bryant.
18. According to the *Monk of Westminster*.
19. *Ibid.*
20. *Music in Medieval Britain*, Frank le Harrison. He played the flute or recorder.
21. *English Historical Review*, XLII.
22. *Chronicle of Adam of Usk*, Maunde Thompson.
23. *Monk of Westminister*.

Chapter V

1. *English Constitutional Documents*, Lodge and Thornton.
2. *Fourteenth Century Studies*, M.V. Clarke.
3. *The Westminster Chronicle 1381-84*, edited by the late L.C. Hector and Barbara F. Harvey.
4. See MacMichael, N.H., *Sanctuary at Westminster*, Occasional Papers 1970-74.
5. *Monk of Westminster*.
6. *Ibid.*
7. *The Court of Richard II*.
8. *Monk of Westminster*.
9. *The Hollow Crown*, Hutchison.

Chapter VI

1. *Chronicles of Froissart*. Battle of Otterburn (1388).
2. See p. 44, Sidney's *Defence of Poesie*, a limited edition printed in Cambridge.

3. Froissart.
4. *The Hollow Crown*, Hutchison.
5. *Westminster Chronicle 1381-1384*, edited and translated by the late L.C. Hector and Barbara F. Harvey.
6. See p. 361 et seq, *Westminster Chronicle*.
7. *The Hollow Crown*, Hutchison.
8. See *Richard II*, Steel, a note p. 172.
9. *Hist. Anglic*. II, 181.
10. Dictionary of National Biography.
11. Edited by Benjamin Williams.
12. Marie Louise Bruce, *The Usurper King*.
13. *John of Gaunt*, Sydney Armitage Smith.
14. J.R. Green, *History of the English People*, Vol. II (1904), p. 506.
15. *The Royal Policy of Richard II* (1968).
16. Froissart, chapter on Charles VI - how he became mad.
17. *A Distant Mirror*, Barbara W. Tuchman.
18. *Cambridge Medieval History*, vol. 7.

Chapter VII

1. See Steel's *Richard II*.
2. *English Art from 1307-1461*.
3. Edited by Samuel Pegge 1780 and printed by J. Nichols Society of Antiquaries.
4. *The Court of Richard II* by Gervase Mathew.
5. Vol. I, *Medieval London*.
6. *Ibid*.
7. p. 118, *Chronique de la Traison et Mort de Richard II*, edited by Benjamin Williamson.
8. *The Court of Richard II*.
9. Harleian MSS 1319, British Library.
10. *Fourteenth Century Studies*, M.V. Clarke.
11. p. 120, *Fourteenth Century Studies*.
12. F. Palgrave, *Ancient Kalendars and Inventories of the Treasury of the Exchequer (1836)*.
13. John Harvey, *The Plantagenets*, p. 153.
14. Bishop Stubbs, Vol. I, p. 534.
15. *Edward II* by Harold F. Hutchison, p. 153.
16. He succeeded Pope Urban VI.
17. Henry Yevele built two spiral staircases at Kennington.
18. *The Court of Richard II*.
19. *History of the King's Works*, Vol. I, p. 550. Edward's clerk of works paid Robert Foundeur 56s 8d for two large bronze taps for the king's bath.
20. A modern building in Court Road is now occupied by the Directorate of Army Education.
21. p. 156, *Westminster Chronicle*.
22. *History of the King's Works*, Vol. 2.
23. Vol. 2, p. 1006.

24. E.W. Tristam, *English Wall Paintings of the Fourteenth Century*.
25. Shakespeare, *Henry IV*, Part II. Rumour.
26. British Library, Royal MS. I.E. IX.
27. Trinity Hall, Cambridge, MS.17.
28. M.S. Queen's College, Oxford, MS 2133.
    Magrath, *The Queen's College, Oxford* (1921), pp. 118 and 119.
29. An original copy printed at London in Fleet Street by Thomas Rerthelette.
30. *The Court of Richard II*, Gervase Mathew.
31. *The Portable Chaucer*, revised edition, edited and translated by Theodore Morrison.
32. Née Katherine Roet.
33. *A Study in Early Fifteenth Century Poetic*, Jerome Mitchell.
34. *Le Male Regle*.
35. *De Regimine Principium*, written in the regin of Henry IV and edited by Thomas Wright (Roxburghe Club).
36. See Nigel Saul's article, vol. 37, *History Today* (November 1987).

Chapter VIII

1. *The Turbulent London of Richard II* by Ruth Bird.
2. Higden, IX, 267-70, also Hutchison's *The Hollow Crown*.
3. *The Turbulent London of Richard II*, p. 104.
4. *The Brut* or *The Chronicles of England*, edited from MS., Rawlinson, B.171. Bodleian Library by Friedrich W.D. Brie, see p. 345.
5. *Ibid*.
6. *Ibid*.
7. *John of Gaunt* by Armitage-Smith.
8. *Ibid*.
9. Marie Louise Bruce, *The Usurper King* (1986).
10. *Ibid*.
11. Westminster Abbey Manuscripts, MS. 23970 B.
12. p. 348.
13. Westminster Abbey Manuscripts, MS. 5257 A.
14. *Richard II in Ireland 1394-95* by Dr. Edmund Curtis (1927).
15. *Ibid*. Edmund Curtis.
16. *The Hollow Crown*, Hutchison.
17. Proceedings of the Royal Irish Academy, vol. XXVII. Unpublished letters of Richard II in Ireland. All Souls' MSS. Oxford Letters translated by Edmund Curtis.
18. *Ibid*.
19. See Letter 5. Fol. 255R-255V. Letters are in French.
20. *Ibid*. Proceedings of the Royal Irish Academy, Vol. XXVII.
21. Formerly in the household of Queen Anne.
22. *English Historical Review CCI* (1936).
    Heresy and the Lay Power, H.C. Richardson.
23. *The Hollow Crown*.
24. *Fourteenth Century Studies*, M.V. Clarke.
25. Rymer, *Foedera VII*, 811.
26. 229A, June 1396, Richard II in a letter to Charles VI.

27. *The Hollow Crown*, p. 163.
28. *The Brut*, p. 350.

Chapter IX

1. Steel's *Richard II*, pp. 174 and 175.
2. John Harvey's *The Plantagenets*.
3. *Westminster Abbey Official Guide*.
4. *Adam of Usk Chronicle*, p. 169.
5. D.N.B. edited by Leslie Stephen.
6. *Chronique de La Traison*, pp. 2 and 119.
7. *La Traison*, pp. 4 and 123. *Ibid.*
8. Steel, see p. 230.
9. In the reign of Henry VI known as Poultney's Inn. The house once belonged to Michael de la Pole, earl of Suffolk.
10. See *An English Chronicle of the Reigns of Richard II, Henry IV, Henry V, and Henry VI* by Rev. John Silvester Davis.
11. *The Hollow Crown*, Hutchison.
12. *The Kirkstall Abbey Chronicle*, edited by John Taylor, M.A., p. 74.
13. *Ibid.*, p. 75.
14. *Ibid.*, p. 75.
15. July 12th 1397.
16. Steel's analysis of the evidence, p. 239.
17. See A.E. Stamp's convincing article, *English Historical Review*, XXXVIII.
18. *The History of England* by Dr. John Lingard, Vol. III, p. 366.
19. See pp. 11 and 140, *Chronique de la Traison*.

Chapter X

1. In the act legitimating the Beauforts.
2. *L'Angleterre et le Grand Schisme* (1933), E. Perroy.
3. *The Kirkstall Abbey Chronicles*, pp. 75 and 119.
4. *The Hollow Crown*, Hutchison.
5. Steel's opinion that the Welshman was a pushing vulgar attorney without principle or scruple may be too strong, but Adam was dishonest on occasions and capable of treachery, if it suited his purpose. His Chronicle is of value because he is often an eye-witness of exciting events.
6. pp. 12 and 141, *La Traison*. See also *Kirkstall Chronicle*.
7. *The Usurper King*, Marie Louise Bruce, p. 176.
8. *The Brut*, Lambeth Edition.
9. pp. 18 and 149, *La Traison*.
10. *Henry IV*, Part II.
11. *Chronique de la Traison*, note p. 160.
12. *Calendar of the Patent Rolls*, October 3rd 1398.
13. *Henry IV*, Part I, Scene 3.
14. All the Chronicles mention Richard's extravagance.
15. *Richard Whittington*, pp. 205, 209 and 210 by Caroline Barron.
16. *Ibid.*
17. *Annales Ricardi II et Henrici IV. Richard II*, Steel.
18. *Political Poems and Songs*, edited Wright, p. 363.

19. The Duke of Lancaster is buried with his first wife in St. Paul's.
20. *The Hollow Crown*, Hutchison.
21. Her younger sister Philippa had married Robert de Vere, Earl of Oxford.

Chapter XI

1. See MSS 1319 (Harleian), British Library, also *Histoire du roy d'Angleterre Richard*, edited and translated by John Webb, Archaeological Society of Antiquaries (1824).
2. *Ibid.*, MSS 1319, Harleian; see also *Henry V*, Desmond Seward (1987).
3. *Ibid.*, MSS 1319.
4. His name is remembered for the beautiful gateway to Norwich Cathedral.
5. Monk of Evesham said that he landed about the feast of St. John the Baptist (July 1st).
6. *Chronique de la Traison*, pp. 180 and 181.
7. *Annales de Ricardi II and Henrici IV*, pp. 239 and 240.
8. *Hardyng's Chronicle*.
9. See Créton, *Histoire du Roy d'Angleterre* edited and translated by John Webb, Archaeological Society of Antiquaries, p. 551.
10. *History of England*.
11. *Fourteenth Century Studies*, p. 67.
12. *Chester in the Plantagenet and Tudor Reigns* by Rupert H. Morris, p.35. See also *Early History of the Leghs*, Chapter I. The Black Prince had given Piers Legh and Margaret his wife land called Hawley or Lyme Hanley. Peter Legh of Lyme buried in the Church of the Carmelite Friars.
13. pp. 46 and 194, *Chronique de la Traison*.
14. Article by Professor Wilkinson, *English Historical Review*, January - October 1939, vol. 54.
15. According to the *Chronique de la Traison*, pp. 49 and 198.
16. *Harleian* MSS 1319. Illustration opposite folio 42. Northumberland in blue gown and gold stars taking the oath in Chapel of Conway Castle.
17. *Chronique de la Traison*, p. 201.
18. *Hardyng's Chronicle*, p. 352.
19. *The Reign of Richard II*, edited by F.R.H. Du Boulay and Caroline M. Barron (1971).
20. In Henry IV's first Parliament Chester reverted from the status of a principality to that of a county. See Du Boulay and Barron.
21. *Chronique de la Traison*, pp. 61 and 211.
22. *Ibid.*, pp. 66 and 217.
23. See Steel's *Richard II*.

Chapter XII

1. *Adam of Usk*, pp. 30 and 182.
2. Shakespeare's *Richard II*, Act III, Scene II:
   'For God's sake, let us sit upon the ground,
   and tell sad stories of the deaths of kings.'
3. And also in the Rot. Parl., Vol. III, 417-22.

The Hollow Crown, pp. 228 and 229.

4. Du Boulay and Barron, *The Reign of Richard II, 1388-99*. See chapter V, English Foreign Policy.

5. Rot. Parl. III, 422-23.

6. pp. 70 and 71. Also pp. 221 and 222.

7. *The Usurper King*, Marie Louise Bruce.

8. Colchester had accompanied King Richard in 1399 to Ireland.

9. *La Traison* account mentions 8,000 archers would be used, probably a grossly exaggerated figure.

10. His father is commemorated in Westminster Abbey.

11. Shakespeare also relates how Aumerle (Rutland) confessed the plot to King Henry. Rutland fought at Agincourt where he was killed.

12. *The Hollow Crown.*

Bibliography

Adam of Usk Chronicon (1377-1404), ed. E. Maunde Thompson (with translation), London, 1904.
Annales Ricardi II et Henrici IV (1392-1406) in Chronica Johannis de Trokelowe, ed. H.T. Riley (Rolls Series).
Anon. Chronica, *The Anonimalle Chronicle (1333-1381)*, ed. V.H. Galbraith, 1927.
Armitage-Smith, S., *John of Gaunt*, London, 1904.
Aston, M.E. (Miss), *Thomas Arundel*, Oxford, 1967.
Barron, Caroline M., *Richard Whittington*.
Bean, M.W., *Henry IV and the Percies*, 1959.
Besant, Sir Walter, *Medieval London*, Vol. I.
Betts, R., Professor, *Transactions of the Royal Historical Society*, Fourth Series, Volume XXI, 1939.
English and Czech Influences on the Hussite Movement.
Bird, Ruth, *The Turbulent London of Richard II*, London, 1949.
Bruce, Marie Louise, *The Usurper King*, 1986.
The Brut or the Chronicle of England, ed. F.W.D. Brie. Early English Text Society. Orig. Series 36, 1985.
Bryant, Sir Arthur, *Set in a Silver Sea.*
Cambridge Medieval History of England, Vol. VII.
Calendar of the Patent Rolls, 1377-1381, Vol. VII, 609.
Capgrave, John, *The Chronicle of England.*
Chaucer, Geoffrey, *The Poetical Works*, ed. F.N. Robinson, 1933.
The Portable Chaucer, edited and translated Theodore Morris.
Clarke, M.V., *Fourteenth Century Studies*, ed. L.S. Sutherland and M. McKissack, Oxford, 1937.
Colvin, H.M., *History of the King's Works*, Vols. I, II, III, IV.
Chronique de la Traison et Mort de Richard II, English Historical Society 12, ed. Benjamin Williams, 1846.
Coulton, G.L., *Mediaeval Panorama*, Cambridge, 1938.
Créton, Jean, *Histoire du Roy d'Angleterre Richard*, ed. & trans. John Webb.
Curtis, E., *Richard II in Ireland*, Oxford, 1927.
Curtis, E., Proc. R. Irish Academy XXXVII, Sec. C, no. 14.
Davies Chron., *An English Chronicle of the Reigns of Richard II, Henry IV*, ed. Rev. J.S. Davies.
Camden orig. series 64 (1856).
Dictionary of National Biography (DNB) edited by Leslie Stephen.
The Dieulacres Chronicle, ed. M.V. Clarke and V.H. Galbraith.
Daviot, Gordon, *Richard of Bordeaux*, a play, 1932.
The Diplomatic Correspondence of Richard II, ed. E. Perroy, Camden 3rd series XLVIII.
Dos Passos, John, *The Portugal Story*, 1933.
Dugdale's Baronage II.
Du Boulay and Barron (ed.), *The Reign of Richard II*. Essays in honour of May McKisack, 1971.
Duls, Louise, *Richard II in the Early Chronicles*, (The Hague, 1975).
Earle, Peter, *The Life and Times of Henry V*, 1972. *The Black Prince*, 1972.

English Historical Review by N.B. Lewis, pp. 402-407.

Evans, Joan, Dr., *English Art 1307-1461*, Oxford, 1949.

Favent, Thomas, *Historia Mirabalis Parliament* MCCCLXXXVI, ed. by Mary McKisack.

The Forme of Cury, ed. Samuel Pegge, Society of Antiquaries, (1780).

Froissart, Jean, *Chroniques*, ed. K. de Lettenhove (Brussels) 1867-77, also trans. Lord Berners, ed. W.P. Ker, 6 vols.,(London 1901-03).

Froissart Chronicles selected. Translated and edited Geoffrey Brereton, 1968.

Formulary book preserved in the Library of All Souls College Oxford relating to Richard II's first expedition to Ireland.

Gower, John, *The Complete Works*, ed. G.C. Macaulay, 2 vols. *Vox Clamantis*, Book I. *De Confessione Amantis*, Thomas Rerthelette.

Green, J.R. & Norgate, *A Short History of the English People*, Vol. 2.

Hardyng Chronicle. Chronicle of John Hardyng, ed. Henry Ellis, 1812.

Harrison, F. le, *Music in Medieval Britain*, ed. Henry Ellis, 1812.

Harvey, John, *The Plantagenets*, London, 1948. *Henry Vevele*, 1944.

Hector, L.C. *English Historical Review*, LXVIII.

Hoccleve, Thomas, *De Regimine Principium*, London, 1976. *The Minor Poems* (1892), ed. F.J. Furnivall.

Hutchinson, Harold F., *The Hollow Crown*, London, 1961. *Edward II, The Pliant King*, 1971.

Holinshed, *Chronicles of England. Chronicles of Scotland.*

Jolliffe, *Constitutional History of Medieval England.*

Johnson, Paul, *The Life and Times of Edward III*, 1973.

Jones, R.H., *The Royal Policy of Richard II*, 1968.

The Kirkstall Chronicle 1355-1400, ed. Clarke and Denholm-Young, 1931.

Knighton Chronicle, Henrici Knighton, ed. J.R. Lumby, 2 Vols., Rolls Series, 1895.

Lawrence, Hannah, *Historical Memoirs of the Queens of England*, Vol. II, pp. 222, 238.

Langland, William, *The Vision of Piers Plowman*, ed. W.W. Skeat, Oxford, 1886 and Everyman edition.

Lingard, John, *History of England*, III, London, 1823.

Lodge, E.C. and Thornton, G.A., *English Constitutional Documents 1307-1485*, Cambridge, 1935.

McFarlane, K.B., *Lancastrian Kings and Lollard Knights*, Oxford, 1972.

MacMichael, N.H., *Sanctuary at Westminster* (W.A. Muniments).

Macrath, Vol. I, *The Queen's College*, Oxford, 1921.

Mathew, Gervase, *The Court of Richard II*, Cambridge, 1962.

Mitchell, Jerome, *Thomas Hoccleve, a study in Early Fifteenth Century Poetic.*

Monk of St. Albans. See Thomas Walsingham.

Monk of Evesham, *Historia Vitae et Regni Ricardi Secundo*, ed. Thomas Hearne, 1729.

Monk of St. Denys, *Chronique du Religieux de Saint Denys 1380-1422*, trans. M.L. Bellanquet.

Myres, J.N.L., 'The Campaign of Radcot Bridge in December 1387', EHR XLII, 1927.

Neale, John Preston, *A History and Antiquities of the Abbey Church of St. Peter Westminster*, Vol. I.

Oman, C., *Political History of England*, Vols. I, II, III and IV.

Oman, C., *The Great Revolt of 1381.*

Palgrave, F., *Ancient Kalendars and Inventories of the Treasury of the Exchequer*, 1836, Vol. III.

Palmer, J., *English Foreign Policy 1388-99*, du Boulay and Barron, 1971.

Palmer, J., *Political Characters of Shakespeare*.

Pegge, Samuel, (ed.) *The Forme of Cury*, 1780.

Richardson, H. and C., *English Historical Review. Heresy and the Lay Power*. No. CCI, January 1936.

Salzman, L.F., *English Life in the Middle Ages*, Oxford, 1941.

Select Documents of English Constitutional History 1307-1485, ed. and trans. S.B. Chrines and A.L. Brown, London, 1961.

Senior, Michael, *The Life and Times of Richard II*, 1981.

Seward, Desmond, *Henry V as Warlord*, 1986.

Shakespeare, William, *King Richard II. King Henry IV*, Part I.

Stamp, A.E., 'Richard II and the Death of the Duke of Gloucester', *EHR* XXXVIII, 1923.

Steel, Anthony, *King Richard II*, Cambridge, 1962.

Stow, John, *The Chronicles of England*, London 1580.

Strickland, Agnes, *Lives of the Queens of England from the Norman Conquest*, Vol. I. Anne of Bohemia, pp. 591-614.

Stubbs, Bishop, *Constitutional History*, Vol. II, 1887.

Tout, T.F., Chapters in the *Administrative History of Medieval England*, Manchester, Vols. II and III.

Trevelyan, G.M., *England in the Age of Wycliffe*.

Tuchman, Barbara W., *A Distant Mirror*.

Tuck, J.A., 'The Cambridge Parliament', *English Historical Review*, April 1969, p. 225.

Tristam, E.W., *English Wall Paintings of the Fourteenth Century*, 1955.

Wallon, Henri, *Richard II*, Tome I and II, Paris, 1864.

Walsington, Thomas, *Historia Anglicana Annales Richard II*.

The Westminster Chronicle 1381-1394, edited and translated by the late L.C. Hector and Barbara F. Harvey, 1982.

Woods, William, *England in the Age of Chaucer*, 1976.

Wright, H.G., 'Richard II and the Duke of Gloucester', *EHR* XLVII, 1932.

Wright's *Political Poems I and II and Songs, Rolls Series, 1859-61*.

Wylie, J.H., *History of England under Henry IV*, Vols. 1 and 2, 1884-98.

Manuscripts

Alnwick MSS. Alnwick Castle.

Bodley MS.581, fol. 9 and fol. 87. Bodley MS.294.

British Library. Royal MS. IEX, IX, Fol. 229.   Great Bible of Richard II.

Harleian MS.1319 contains *Histoire du Roy Richard* written in French verse by Jean Créton.

Trinity Hall, Cambridge 17. *The Book against the twelve errors of heresie of the Lollards* by the Court Dominican Roger Dymock.

MSS in Westminster Abbey Muniments.:

MSS.5157. Grant from Richard II to William Colchester Abbot, the prior and Convent of Westminster.

MSS.5431. Concerns the election of William Colchester to be Abbot.

MSS.4498, MSS.12699 and MS.12694, MS.32778. Complaint by William Colchester to the King against Richard Beauchamp Earl of Warwick for interfering as Sheriff of Worcester with the liberties and franchises granted to Abbot's predecessors by St. Edward the Confessor and his successors.

W.A. Draft. Letters Patent of Manumission and Pardon for Men of Somerset in 1381.

MS Queen's College, Oxford, MS.2133.

178

Index

182